Philosophical Variations:
Music as 'Philosophical Language'

ANDREW BOWIE

Philosophical Variations:
Music as 'Philosophical Language'

NSU SUMMERTALK **VOL. 5** | 2010

An NSU Series Edited by:
Claus Krogholm

NSU Press

Contents

Introduction

Philosophy today is widely thought of as divided up into distinct areas, such as metaphysics, semantics, philosophy of mind, aesthetics, etc., in which specific problems are examined by detailed conceptual analysis and the building of specific arguments. However, one of the effects of this approach is to create ever more specialised subdivisions, to which less and less people can contribute, given the accumulation of specialised assumptions to which the practitioners in each area subscribe. An analogous situation is present in the natural sciences, but there the results of the specialisation can, unlike in philosophy, rapidly feed into technological, medical, and other practices that change things for non-specialists. In the face of this situation one has to ask what the aim of such specialised philosophising can be, given that a) the likelihood of widespread consensus on the results is so small, and b) the results will be effectively inaccessible to most of the wider culture. It is a notorious fact that those working in humanities departments in the English-speaking world, who often have a deep interest in philosophy, often say that they find it impossible to discuss anything serious with many of their colleagues from philosophy departments. This may be the fault of those in the humanities for failing to engage with the cutting-edge developments in philosophy, but there are serious reasons to doubt this.

One way – there are many – of pondering what is at stake here is to think how what one does philosophically relates to the rest of one's approach to life. The occasional essays which form the present volume document the author's growing sense that what I initially thought of as separate intellectual and existential compartments in my life, in which, for example, my professional philosophical and literary concerns bore little relation to my love for playing and listening to music, have to be connected if the theories in one area are not to be contradicted by practice in another, and vice versa. The change of attitude that has resulted does not, I hope, invalidate the philosophical work which I have done over the years, which has tended to relate to issues in aesthetics and the history of philosophy, nor has it diminished my musical passions (though it has forced me to take my music-making more seriously, with some benefit to my jazz playing). What it has done above all is to convince me that much specialised philosophical theorising, by the very fact that it is often nearly impossible to connect it to social and cultural concerns, should be considered less in terms of its possible truth value (which will necessarily be contended), than in terms of its contribution to making sense of the modern world in ways which feed into the wider culture. Such a stance should be familiar from the work of Dewey, Rorty, and others: what I seek to offer here are some different perspectives on such approaches to the practice of philosophy.

Whereas most contemporary analytical approaches regard aesthetics as a separate, comparatively insignificant, philosophical domain, I think more and more that the issues raised by aesthetics are germane to what matters most in modern philosophy. Such a contention cannot be legitimated by any kind of decisive argument, of the kind which would prove how aesthetics is essential to the questions of language, metaphysics, or whatever, which form the main focus of analytical philosophy. The contention can only be defended by actually engaging with key issues in modernity, and in my case one central focus here is on the role of music. The reason I do not think there is such a decisive argument is that the search for it would already lead one into the styles of philosophising which generate the problems suggested above. It is not that in adopting the kind of approach suggested here that one renounces the practice of argumentation, but part of the point of aesthetics is that it both demands justificatory argument and suggests the limits of what can be actually achieved by argument (for the classic statement on this issue see Stanley Cavell's 'Aesthetic Problems of Modern Philosophy' (in *Must we mean what we say?*, (Cambridge: Cambridge University Press 1976)).

The underlying idea here is simply that aesthetics offers a reminder that 'meaning' is not something that can be reduced to a philosophical theory, such as the versions of semantics which have dominated much analytical philosophy, to the frequent exclusion of all the other forms of articulation which enable us to make sense of our world. What has largely been excluded in this way has, I think, considerable implications for philosophy. Given the contemporary lack of a unified philosophical agenda, in which the key philosophical problems and the manner in which they are to be addressed would be substantially agreed upon, the choice of stance with regard to what one does philosophically cannot be assumed to be unproblematically given. Insistence on an agenda dictated by some conception of tradition (and how many of those are there?), in which philosophy, as Kant suggested, for example, is about what we can know, what we should do, and – at this point the way tradition changes with history becomes very apparent – what we can hope for, cannot just appeal to tradition for its legitimation. Even in those areas which assume an agenda dictated by the traditional concerns of the analytic approach philosophers address themselves to a limited number of peers who have established a way of working on certain issues, and do not discuss (or often even read) other philosophers' work which probably involves some of the same themes, but deals with them in a different manner. Given the proliferation of philosophical approaches this is, of course, inevitable (though one is often shocked by the parochialism of some philosophers with regard to issues that are necessarily connected to their field of research). What is really so often missing is, though, at least some kind of meta-reflection on the element of contingency involved in the adoption of a philosophical stance and a peer group, in the face of the massive divergences among the available stances.

The contingency in question here can, of course, also often turn out to involve a substantial amount of ideology. The exclusion of Hegel from the empiricist-dominated analytical agenda, for example, cannot, in the light of the recent return of Hegelian issues, be seen as having been justified by stringent, decisive argument, even though it was an accepted norm for much of analytical philosophy for much of the twentieth century. The first question here has to be to ask just why it was that such a stance became so dominant, which is not a question purely internal to philosophical argument. The lack of conclusive arguments in philosophy is significantly at odds with the manner in which much philosophy is presented: arguments, especially in the analytical tradition, are frequently put forward with an appearance of certainty that jars with the awareness that history has shown how provisional or partial philosophical arguments turn out to be. It took until quite recently for anyone committed to the analytical tradition to take seriously the fact that the tradition had a history which is part of its content in the same way as it is in any other intellectual enterprise. It is no use here suggesting that the arguments are necessary stages in some kind of cumulative philosophical progress: why would it be that so many philosophers now see the need to 'go back to Kant' if that were the case? It is anyway unclear what the criteria for philosophical progress really are, and the assumption is too often that it just consists in refuting arguments, with no further reflection on the value of what has been achieved in this way.

Consideration of issues central to aesthetics in this context derives from the assumption that the starting point for philosophical theories cannot itself be grounded and so will also depend on judgements about the relevance of the issues to which one devotes one's philosophical time. Relevance cannot be established by argument alone, because it involves complexes of background assumptions which cannot all be brought to light in the form of explicit premises. This basic hermeneutic point makes it clear that judgements on the adoption of philosophical stances need not differ greatly from those involved in aesthetic judgements. The recent claims by Timothy Williamson and others that we can return to solving metaphysical problems need not, in this perspective, be countered by arguments against the specifics of their case, but can instead be countered by questions about what such theorising is supposed to achieve. The idea that philosophy can 'discover what fundamental kinds of things there are and what properties and relations they have' (Williamson 2007 p. 19) can be more effectively questioned by suggesting that the modern world has shown that the natural sciences' ways of doing this have a rather better record than philosophy's, than by an attempt to formulate a philosophical argument to deny the claim. One can, in short, make a judgement, based on relevance, that one simply does not wish to pursue this sort of philosophical agenda, in the way that one judges certain forms of cultural production to be not worth taking seriously or to be culturally damaging.

So what approaches are adopted in the following essays? They can be illustrated by an example which has been decisive for my work, culminating in the recent *Music, Philosophy, and Modernity* (Cambridge University Press 2007). The obvious assumption would be that this is a book about the 'Philosophy of Music', but this is only the case in a specific sense. Rather than give philosophy the privileged position with respect to music, a position which is contradicted by the relative contemporary significance of philosophy and music as cultural practices, where music clearly plays a much greater role in most peoples' lives, the book experiments with the idea of the philosophy of music in the 'subjective genitive', in the sense of the philosophy which ensues from music, or which is embodied in music. The question is what can music tell us about philosophy, rather than vice versa. The prima facie implausibility of this approach can be countered by considering the fact that there is a significant strand of modern philosophy from the early Romantics, to Schopenhauer, Nietzsche, and Wittgenstein, who took such an approach seriously. The aim is not to ignore thoughts about the Philosophy of Music in the objective genitive, but rather to see what they neglect or repress, and what this means for our understanding of the role of philosophy in modernity. If people look for meaning in their lives of a non-theological kind, they often realise it in a practice like music, rather than in thinking in terms of ideas about life. The kind of reversal suggested by this example involves an approach to philosophy which sees it as a practice of making connections that can generate new kinds of meaning, rather than as a source of theoretical responses to the supposed 'perennial' philosophical questions. It is not that the perennial problems – whether they are really the same problems is, of course, open to dispute – are ignored, but they are looked at in a dual perspective, both as issues that need to be argued about, and as expressions of historical tensions that relate to issues studied in other areas of the humanities and the sciences. This stance is in line with some of the more important developments in the humanities in recent years, which have sought to break down boundaries between different disciplines. The idea that the crucial role for philosophy is to make new connections, rather than seek answers to foundational metaphysical questions, is essential to the neglected philosophy of early German Romanticism, which prefigures key aspects of American pragmatism, and forms the implicit and explicit background to many of the essays.

The papers stem from a period of something over ten years, and some repeat ideas and brief passages from already published work, but they can stand on their own as they each address some way of suggesting new perspectives on an issue. The first paper was given in 2004 at 'Continental Drift? Modern European Philosophy in Britain Today', a conference of the Middlesex University Centre for Research in Modern European Philosophy'; the second was given at the University of East Anglia in 2002 at a conference of the Society for Musical Analysis on 'Music and Ethics'; the third was given in 1997 at the Royal Festival Hall before a concert in Maurizio Pollini's Beethoven Sonatas series; the fourth was first given at the Royal Academy of Music 'Performance Perspectives' Lecture Series in 1998; the fifth was given at a Conference on 'Shakespeare and Philosophy in a Multicultural World' at the Loránd Eötvös University of Budapest in 2003; the sixth at a conference on 'The Philosophy of the History of Philosophy' at the University of Southern Denmark, Odense 2002; the seventh, which forms a kind of 'satyr play' in relation to the rest

– sometimes philosophy can be understood as a performative activity – at the inaugural conference of the Society for European Philosophy at the University of Lancaster in 1998. All the papers have been revised and some have been expanded, but I have not tried to make them all fully consistent with my present-day ideas on the issues.

Music, Meaning, and Philosophy

Asked to say what differentiates 'Continental' or 'European' philosophy from analytical philosophy, the average analytical philosopher would, if polite, probably say that it involved a greater awareness of historical issues, but that it tended to avoid the detailed work required to establish serious philosophical arguments. If they were not so polite they would say that Continental philosophy was not really philosophy at all, being at best a version of the history of ideas, and at worst a subject obsessed with the texts of a few often obscure master thinkers, at the expense of real 'philosophical' engagement with real problems. The polite Continental philosopher would admire the persistence and frequent clarity with which arguments are pursued in the analytical tradition, but would be concerned at its lack of awareness of the situated historical nature of the practice of philosophy. They might also doubt that many of the problems whose solutions are sought in that tradition are really significant problems at all, being, as they are, generated by the untenable empiricist model that seeks to connect an 'inside' mind and an 'outside' world. The less polite Continental philosopher would claim that analytical philosophy was still 'stuck in the metaphysics of presence/representation', and that it failed to address the deep cultural crises which arise from the demise of 'Western metaphysics'. The idea of crisis associated with the demise of 'metaphysics' – a term whose meaning in one tradition is sometimes the opposite of what it is in the other: for the Vienna Circle it can be anything that is not empirically verifiable, for the later Heidegger it becomes natural science itself – points to a question that should be addressed to both sides of this imagined altercation. I say 'imagined', because the very existence of such a division generally has more to do with institutionalised disciplinary contingencies than with the substantive questions themselves.

With regard to the division between the traditions Samuel Wheeler usefully suggests, in his excellent *Deconstruction as Analytical Philosophy*, that some of the division is a result of the extent to which 'philosophical notions' are perceived to infect the rest of culture' (Wheeler 2000 p. 71). The way of investigating this question I want to propose here is in terms of approaches to 'meaning' in the respective traditions. The first thing to remember here is that most people are well aware of problems concerning meaning in everyday communication, but that does not entail that one can construct a 'philosophical' position concerning culture in general from such awareness. Whether we think of true sentences as corresponding to reality, or as being well-confirmed, or as being those that best cohere with other truths has little directly to do with how people have to engage with truth in their everyday lives.

To make it clear what I mean, let's take a well-known example, which seeks to construct a philosophical position concerning meaning which sees it as infecting the rest of culture. In *The Origins of the German Play of Mourning* (1928), Walter Benjamin says of the incidence of allegory in the baroque period in Germany – and the same largely applies to the Shakespearean period in Britain – that 'Every person, every thing, every relationship can arbitrarily mean something else. This possibility passes a devastating but just judgement on the profane world: it is characterised as a world in which details are not strictly that important' (Benjamin GS I 1 p. 350). Even if nothing in Benjamin's overall argument could really be called simple, the simple inference from this has to be that there used to be a sacred world in which things' meanings were not arbitrary. His remark elsewhere that 'As humankind steps out of the pure language of the name it makes language into a means (namely of a cognition which is inappropriate to it), thereby in one part at least into a *mere* sign .... the origin of abstraction as a capacity of the spirit of language may also be sought in the Fall' (ibid. p. 152–4) suggests the theological underpinning of his position reasonably clearly. Allegory and related phenomena, like Shakespearean word-play – given Benjamin's specific characterisation here they cannot be separated – in which meanings are not fixed, become for Benjamin indications of the problematic nature of the development of modernity.

Now let's think of the basic idea here another way. One view of post-structuralism might be that it tells a similar story in a different frame, with the evaluation inverted. Whereas the preceding assumed state of non-arbitrariness is positively assessed in basically theological terms by Benjamin, in post-structuralism that state could be seen as the very essence of 'logocentrism', 'ontotheology', and the 'metaphysics of presence', in which signification relies on the idea of a substantial correspondence of some kind between signifier and signified. Once the shifting relationality of the material of signification and the temporality of those relations is appreciated, the world of stable meanings dissolves. In his melodramatic, Nietzschean mode, Derrida, at the end of 'Structure, Sign, and Play', sees this as having epochal *philosophical* significance, as the end of the dream of metaphysics as 'presence', with all sorts of exciting consequences. However, I'm not so sure of either Benjamin's or Derrida's justifications for their emphatic stance. What makes Wheeler's account of the issue notable is that he shows how the basic thought in question, i.e. the idea that there are no such things as 'meanings', in the sense of wholly stable links between word and object, need not be that dramatic. As Wheeler puts it: 'If there are no magical, naturally referring words, then meaning is nothing deeper than uses of ordinary words in particular circumstances' (Wheeler 2000 p. 63). This idea is shared by Wittgenstein, Davidson, Rorty, and many others, and it was already developed as part of the modern hermeneutic tradition established by Schleiermacher, who first rejected the analytic/synthetic distinction in exactly the manner that later enabled Quine to put in question empiricist theories of meaning (see Bowie 2003 Chapter Six).

There is, then, an important division here, at the level of the perceived consequences for philosophy of giving up the search for 'meanings', at least in the often rather limited sense of the word in some areas of modern philosophy. Before reflecting on these consequences I want to ask a historical question of Benjamin's version of the story of the demise of meanings. Patricia Parker has argued that Shakespeare's language has to be understood in terms of its location in 'a period when English was not yet standardised into a fixed orthography, obscuring on the printed page the homophonic networks possible before such boundaries were solidified' (Parker 1996 p. 1). German was, of course, also notoriously lacking in standardisation of spelling and usage until Herder and others set about establishing them in the eighteenth century. The homophonic networks Parker refers to are based on the ways in which words that are later assumed to be semantically distinct are semantically linked because of their similar sound. She cites Margareta de Grazia's example that '"beare" was a spelling of "bier"/"coffin", as well as the animal "bear": "borne" – the spelling in the Folio for both "born" or "birthed" and "carried" or "transported" – was capable of multiple meanings in this single spelling, which more modern English has separated into "born" and "borne"' (e-mail communication). De Grazia points out that even talking of puns in this context is questionable because a pun joins two conceptually separate words, when the evidence suggests that the clear conceptual separation itself may only come about when the spelling is standardised. Such usages are, then, characteristic of a 'culture not as dominantly monolingual as later periods or as fixed in its sense of the boundaries between words' (Parker 1996 p. 17), or, for that matter, of the boundaries between things.

Parker sees this state of the culture as something that is then over-taken by a more regimented establishing of linguistic boundaries, one consequence of which is the relegation of women and other 'marginal subjects' to an inferior social status. There is, therefore, no universal gain involved in lexical and semantic stability, though it may have very con-siderable advantages for practices in the natural sciences or in aspects of law. It would not be surprising, then, and this will become important in a moment, if some kind of counter-movement emerged together with a process of standardisation that sought to cater for what was previously articulated in 'homophonic networks'. I am referring, of course, in a very broad sense to 'music'. I don't know enough to see how this is played out in the English context – though the role of Handel in British cultural life would seem to be important here – but Benjamin suggests precisely what I mean with regard to Germany. At the end of the 17th century the separation of sound and meaning, which he sees as part of the separation of the word from a metaphysical order of meaning, means that music becomes 'the opponent of speech, which is loaded with meaning', and this leads, he maintains, to the 'dissolution of *Trauerspiel* into opera' (GS I 1. p. 385) as 'product of the decay' of *Trauerspiel*. Whatever the exact historical interpretation there seems little doubt that one can say that the way music is perceived and the way musical techniques and resources develop relate in this sense to the ways in which language and meaning are understood and regulated.

In Parker's version of the initial story, then, there is no Benjaminian fall from a notionally preferable stable state of language, and the lack of boundaries is seen as allowing the kind of celebratory linguistic diversity subsequently advocated in the latter half of the eighteenth century (at a time when, as we shall see, music's status is rapidly changing) by J.G. Hamann, and developed in the twentieth by Mikhail Bakhtin. The 'fall' is, so to speak, in the other direction: linguistic usage moves in the direction of the fixing of the world and this 'passes a different judgement' on aspects of modernity. It seems pretty clear that Parker's analysis of Shakespeare's language is more in tune with what we know about the history of language in modern Europe than Benjamin's claims about allegorisation. Significantly, Benjamin later transfers the same claim about allegory to the idea of the nineteenth century commodity world of Baudelaire's Paris, which he sees as a world of profane arbitrary identifications that involves a 'devaluation of the world of things'. This suggests, as does the fact that the *Trauerspiel* book has a lot to do with German Expressionism, that he was more interested in making a philosophico-historical point than in historical specificity.[1] Interestingly for what will in a moment become my main theme, Adorno, who shares Benjamin's view of the commodity world's effect on language and culture, uses his idea of allegory to criticise Wagner's music dramas. Wagner 'is an allegorist, not least in the fact that everything can mean everything. Figures and symbols play into each other' (Adorno GS 13 p. 96), and this, Adorno maintains, mythologises Wagner's portrayal of human action and its significance.

What we have just considered can be seen as a model, or, for that matter, an allegory, of philosophical approaches to language. The contrasts between suspicion of what can broadly be termed 'dissemination', and the sense that it is a liberation from repressive identification map in certain respects onto the contrast suggested by Charles Taylor between those who follow Frege in the 'designative' search for meanings, and those who follow the various versions of Romantic philosophy which think of language in 'expressive', 'world-disclosive' terms. It should also be apparent, though, that those in the Romantic camp can become involved in another version of the contrast, as is suggested by the relationship of Benjamin and Adorno to Parker's positive assessment of the sort of thing that they find problematic. Furthermore, many from the analytical camp can these days no longer unambiguously be assigned to the designative view. The interpretation of this situation depends therefore in certain respects precisely on the assessment of how philosophical notions 'infect the rest of culture'. Another way of putting this is in terms of a distinction between (1) things which are a problem for some kinds of philosophy, but not for the rest of culture, and (2) things which only become apparent because of the work of philosophers. Both the analytical and the Continental traditions have tended to have their own versions of neglecting, but also of making, this distinction. The distinction would seem in some conceptions of philosophy to require a decisive demarcation

---

[1] I should add that Benjamin does offer a more dialectical view of the issue than the particular remark about the 'profane world' might suggest, but the lurking theology with regard to language recurs throughout his work.

of what belongs to philosophy from what does not, but that would just be a version of (1), because 'philosophy' would have to legislate on its own status, rather than accept that its status may only emerge by success in relation to (2).

We are clearly getting into rather deep water here, so it's time to set a slightly more tractable agenda. Taylor has increasingly framed his ideas in terms of the aim, in the wake of Wittgenstein, Heidegger, and Merleau-Ponty, of moving from (1) to (2), on the basis of a critique of 'representationalism' as the source of many problems belonging to (1). I want to extend some of what he proposes in relation to the issue of music, meaning, and philosophy. The point of this is to exemplify the kind of ways forward there are for philosophy which does not share the goals of the narrower, empiricist-oriented analytical tradition – which too often is stuck in (1) – and which wishes to say something useful about (2) without, as some recent Continental philosophy does, fetishising 'Philosophy' as some kind of source of superior insight. It seems irrelevant to me whether the work in question would then be called 'analytical' or 'Continental'. The reason I want to introduce music into the discussion is to give an example of how the consequences of issues concerning language and meaning manifest themselves in ways which can affect our self-descriptions and forms of orientation in the world. In the absence of a decisive philosophical account of the difference between language and music – an account which would have to rely on representationalism, with music as an object like any other whose connection to the subject is obscure – it is more productive to see how understandings of language and of music relate to each other in modernity than to think in terms of a definitive philosophical theory of the kind offered in the analytical 'philosophy of music'. The objection to so much of what goes on in such philosophy is that it relies on the idea that philosophy can offer answers to questions like 'Does music mean anything?' by employing a 'philosophical' conception of language and meaning. This prejudges the issues because what is being investigated – i.e. 'music' – itself always already poses questions about language and meaning that are likely be excluded by the philosophical assumptions being employed. It is no good assuming that we can use language to determine what music is, if, as is obvious from the divisions within contemporary philosophy, there is no agreement about what language is either (see Bowie 2007).

The evident problem here for an approach that wishes to avoid the paradigmatic trap of the analytical philosophy of music is that one has to give a verbal account of what is in question, and this would appear to vitiate any attempt to put in question purely verbal accounts of language, meaning, and music. However, the rejoinder to this is part of Taylor's argument. The basic point is that the very ability to understand a verbal account of meaning of any kind itself relies on conditions which are themselves not verbal. Taylor uses this hermeneutic and phenomenological argument against Rorty and Davidson, whom he sees as still hanging on to representationalism, even as they claim to 'walk away' from it (Taylor 2002 p. 159). Like Rorty and Davidson, Taylor wants to get rid of the post-Cartesian representationalist 'framework'. He sees this as consisting in the idea 'that our grasp of the world took the form of representations: ideas in the mind or sentences held true' (ibid.). Hence the analytical philosophy of music's idea that there are a series of true beliefs concerning what music means, what a musical work is, whether music 'arouses emotions', etc. that its job is to establish.

The decisive thing for Taylor is that the representationalist framework occludes

> the way in which the representations we frame, and our entire ability to frame them, are underpinned by our ability to cope with the world in a host of ways: from our capacity as bodily beings to make our way around in our surroundings, picking up, using, avoiding and leaning on things to our knowing as social beings how to relate to and interact with friends, strangers, lovers, children, and so on (ibid.)

What he thinks Rorty and Davidson ignore is that these abilities are 'semi- or utterly inarticulate' and that they 'make sense of our explicit thinking and reactions' (ibid.). The explicit conceptual foreground thus relies on the preconceptual background of 'being in the world'. The link to music that can be made here is suggested by Heidegger's pupil, the musicologist Heinrich Besseler, who talks of music as a *'Weise menschlichen Daseins'*, a *'manner/melody of human existence'* (Besseler 1978 p. 45). It is also worth remembering in this connection that the rise of Cartesian representationalism and the associated epistemological dilemmas – that Schelling already saw as the mistaken obsession of modern philosophy – are contemporaneous with Parker's account of the regimentation of language after Shakespeare and the concomitant demise of 'homophonic networks'.

Part of what Taylor seeks to sustain by his version of anti-representationalism is a non-foundational approach to questions of subjectivity and agency. He directs this aim against the residual representationalism in Rorty and Davidson which holds that 'the only inhabitants of the space of reasons are beliefs' (Taylor 2003 p. 169). The simple way to begin to show why music matters here is to think of the issue of normativity, which these days often takes the place of representationalist epistemology. Normativity can be seen predominantly in terms of belief and procedures of justification, which will evidently be verbal: think of Brandom in *Making it Explicit,* or Habermas' idea of 'discourse'. However, 'getting it right' in music or dance in particular often does not rely on verbally articulable rules, but rather on 'showing', and on kinds of tacit agreement known to performers who may not even be able to say *why* this way is right, rather than another way. This kind of preconceptual aspect of our practices is, although not conceptually articulated, anything but primitive, involving a *feeling* for relevance, salience, appropriateness, etc., without which most forms of culture would be inconceivable. No doubt verbalisations are often indispensable to the development and differentiation of this kind of feeling, but the crucial point is that the relationship between the conceptualised and the non-conceptualised goes both ways. In real communication feeling is also indispensable for interpretation of and communication with others, and it often consists in the apprehension of the 'musical' dimension of utterances. Oliver Sacks cites the case of people with aphasia who can often understand, even though they no longer recognise words, by attending to cadences, tone, rhythm, etc., to the point where they may have a greater sense of the affective content of utterances, including mendacious ones, than people without aphasia.

Any analytical semanticist reading or hearing this may despair at the apparent failure to specify the nature of truth-determinate utterance. This would, however, miss the point. That Herder, the source of Taylor's expressivist view, clearly saw the key aspect of semantic conceptions is evident in his concept of 'reflection'. This is what enables one to fore-ground a characteristic of something, to 'see something as something'. This means that the thing can also be seen as something else and that the subject therefore possess a sense of truth which is based on the possibility of disputing ascriptions. Herder's sheep in the *Essay on the Origin of Language* gains its identity by having the characteristic of bleating, which means that it is not some other animal with its own characterising noise. Herder, though, was fully aware of the other dimensions of language which have to do with our essential practical, affective, and sensuous contact with the world, with what is meaningful, rather than just with what has meaning in the stricter semantic sense. The person who says some of the most revealing things on these issues, who was influenced by Herder but went far beyond him, is that often ignored and misunderstood major philosopher of the nineteenth century, Schleiermacher.

Take his following assertion, which suggests a model for thinking about music that does not rely on any kind of definition, because the terms of the assertion are inferentially articulated in a manner which incorporates the historical dimension vital to the widening of the ways in which we think about meaning that I am interested in: 'Song is the indifference of speech, crying, and laughing. Each of these can approach song, but none of them becomes song without ceasing to be what it is'

(Schleiermacher 1931 p. 324). The different relations between the three elements here can only be adequately appreciated by thinking about the ways in which forms of expression and articulation affect each other in different social and historical situations. Schleiermacher reflects on music as what he terms 'free production in sound', and is particularly aware of the importance of musical developments in the nineteenth century in relation to the development of the sciences and of language. He asks: 'How has this direction towards free production in sound (*'Ton'*) been able to expand itself to such an infinity above what is given in nature?' (Schleiermacher 1842 p. 392), and contrasts the historical development of musical instruments as extensions of the human voice with poetry's lack of extensive development of the material of language. Literary language, with a few exceptions, uses the same words as are used in everyday intercourse, and it is the 'musical' form of combination which makes it what it is. Reflections like this would have been highly unlikely prior to the eighteenth century: the explicit, philosophically articulated need for a form of 'free production in sound' seems dialectically related to a sense of verbal language becoming more regimented and instrumentalised. It also relates to the particular socio-political development in Germany, where the failure to realise many individual freedoms led those like Beethoven to channel their desire for freedom into what Martin Geck has termed 'music as philosophy' (Geck 2000 p. 97). Beethoven produces a work that 'does not *represent* sounding philosophy, but *is* it' (ibid. p. 88). His symphonies 'do not just show what music can do in an advanced state of material, but also what it should demand of the material in order to be understood as spirit of the spirit of the time' (ibid. p. 97).

It is phenomena like these that lead Schleiermacher to question, in a manner which is echoed in Taylor's concern with the preconceptual, the primacy of the verbal in thinking about communication:

If we once more consider how one so easily one-sidedly presupposes that the very direction of the individual towards communication is a verbal one (*'eine logische*'), and yet must admit that all musical representation only really has a minimum of verbal content, then a powerful refutation of this assertion lies in this fact, and it follows that there must be a massive intensity in this direction of the human mind to be able to represent itself purely in its mobility, apart from everything verbal ('*abgesehen von allem Logischen*') (Schleiermacher 1842 p. 399–400).

Although he talks about 'the human mind', which might suggest representationalism, the fact is that Schleiermacher explicitly thought of the mind in terms which Heidegger may actually have adopted from him, for instance when he says in *The Christian Faith* that 'our self-consciousness as consciousness of our being in the world or of our being together with the world is a succession of separate feelings of freedom and feelings of dependence' (Schleiermacher 1960 p. 26). On the one hand, Schleiermacher sees the 'direction of the human mind' towards 'representing itself in its mobility' as an anthropological constant, albeit one which differs in degree in its effects within particular cultures; on the other, it also has to do with the development in modernity in which music takes on a new status and new forms because of changes in the understanding of language.

A further dimension of this development is well explored by Geck. The endlessly debated issue of whether Beethoven's use of words in the conclusion of the Ninth Symphony weakens or strengthens the work is not just a musicologists' obsession. It brings to light vital questions about language and philosophy in modernity. The power of Beethoven's wordless other symphonies lies not least in the way in which they can 'say' things which, if verbally articulated, would have a performative effect that diminishes the other dimensions conveyed by the music: 'A cantata with a "revolutionary" text is tantamount to mere political partisanship; a symphony with a purely musical quotation [Geck is referring to Beethoven's citing of the music of the French Revolution] only participates in the revolutionary spirit' (Geck 2000 p. 15). This is apparent in other aspects of communication. Verbal statements of direct affect, as the Romantics realise, tend to move in the direction of irony, which culminates in such phenomena as Heine's move towards simultaneous sentimentality and cynicism. Musical expressions of affect may become ironic, and do so as Romantic musical forms become problematic at the end of the nineteenth century, but they tend to retain their power as direct expressions because musical material, although it undoubtedly also can 'wear out', does so in different ways from words. Geck suggests that Friedrich Schlegel's famous 'greatest tendencies of the age', namely 'The French Revolution, Fichte's *Wissenschaftslehre*, and Goethe's *Meister*' ought to have the Ninth Symphony added to them, and that the latter two, unlike the Ninth, have become increasingly the preserve of specialists. In a similar vein, Bryan Magee tells the story of the dying man who asks to be taken to hear Wagner's *Meistersinger* to hear the famous quintet, whose significance is deeply influenced by Schopenhauer, for one last time, adding 'It is not easy to imagine someone wanting to read just those few pages of Schopenhauer once more before he died' (Magee 2001 p. 255). This might just seem anecdotal and trivially 'Romantic', but I don't think it is. If philosophy is to sustain its concern with the last things, rather than largely ignoring them in favour of sometimes futile technical questions, or seeking to avoid them by some kind of postmodern irony, it would do well to take such things seriously. The very fact that many people in modernity clearly find more resources for 'meaning' in music than they do in philosophy cannot be ignored.

The real philosophical problem here seems to me simple: is philosophy supposed to give a successful explanation of what it is that music achieves, and in what would that success consist? If the source of music's meaning is non-conceptual, having to do with dimensions of subjectivity and being in the world which are conditions of verbal understanding, there can be no philosophical theory that seeks to do it the other way round. This is, though, only a dilemma if one regards music as primarily a philosophical problem, rather than a cultural resource. The philosophical task then ceases to be the pursuit of an answer and becomes the exploration of the ways in which language and music interact in differing situations. One of the most problematic writers on music, Adorno, is also able at his best to exemplify the kind of thing I mean. Adorno says of music that it 'is the impression of mind in the intentionless which reconciles the mind by faithfully reminding it of its own bodily origin' (Adorno 2001 p. 247). 'Music aims at an intentionless language' (Adorno GS 16 p. 252), precisely in the sense that it does not seek to articulate meanings that can be construed as conceptual claims.[2] The crucial word here, though, is 'aims'. Adorno also makes it clear that music can never be fully separated from intentional language: 'Music without all meaning/ intending ('meinen'), the merely phenomenal context of the sounds would acoustically resemble the kaleidoscope. As absolute meaning, on the other hand, it would cease to be music and would mistakenly become language' (ibid.).

Adorno is at his worst when he seeks to make philosophico-historical totalising judgements to legitimate a particular form of music, as though only the form in question has philosophical validity. It is when he is concerned with what philosophy cannot say and with what music says that he takes us somewhere more interesting. This might seem paradoxical, as he still has to say things about music. However, consider the following passage from the texts on musical reproduction, which lives precisely from its pointing to things which can never be finally mediated:

> music is, as it were, the acoustic objectification of facial expression, which perhaps only separated itself from it in the course of history. If 'a shadow passes over a face', an eye opens, lips half-open, then that is closest to the origin of music as well as to expressionless natural beauty, the path of clouds across the sky, the appearance of the first star, the sun's breaking through clouds. Music as it were in the middle between the spectacle of the sky and of the face. That is the basis of the affinity of music to nature poetry (Adorno 2001 p. 237).

---

[2] 'Intention' has here the sense of 'reference' to objects in the world; music should instead express what it can express.

The point here is that the resistance of music to meaning in the sense of reference and identification is what allows it to function as a form of 'world-disclosure' which cannot be achieved solely by language. If we think of philosophy as essentially connected to interpretation, then the crucial issue in its relationship to music lies in the kind of norms which each articulates and makes apparent. Music's importance for Adorno in this respect depends precisely on its resistance to interpretation in 'intentional' terms and in the normative demand that it be adequately reproduced. This is particularly important for contemporary philosophy in relation to the scope of conceptions of language and meaning.

In the context of a discussion of the relationship between musical text and performance Adorno uses in a useful way the idea of Benjamin that I earlier found so problematic, when he talks of the 'historical dual character of music as mime and language. As mimetic it is not purely readable, and is not purely imitable as language. For this reason it splits itself into the ideal of sound and into script, and needs ever renewed exertion to reconcile the divergent elements' (ibid. p. 238). This exertion cannot ever be grasped in solely conceptual terms because it has to do with the kinds of 'mimetic' relations to the world which purely discursive forms cannot articulate, of the kind referred to by Taylor. Crucially Adorno always sees mimesis as in a dialectic with rationality, but 'art, mimesis which has been driven to consciousness of itself, is still bound to the stimulus, to the immediacy of experience; otherwise it would be indistinguishable from science' (Adorno GS 7 p. 385). The essential question is how this 'consciousness of itself' of art relates to philosophical reflection. The kind of answers we give to questions like this should play a significant role in future conceptions of philosophy beyond the divide between the analytical and European traditions.

References

Adorno, T.W. (1997) *Gesammelte Schriften*, (Frankfurt: Suhrkamp) (20 Vols.)

Adorno, T.W. (2001) *Zur Theorie der musikalischen Reproduktion*, (Frankfurt: Suhrkamp)

Benjamin, Walter (1980) *Gesammelte Schriften*, (Frankfurt: Suhrkamp)

Besseler, Heinrich (1978) *Aufsätze zur Musikästhetik und Musikgeschichte*, (Leipzig: Reclam)

Bowie, Andrew (2003) *Aesthetics and Subjectivity: from Kant to Nietzsche*, (Manchester: Manchester University Press)

Bowie, Andrew (2007) *Music, Philosophy, and Modernity*, (Cambridge: Cambridge University Press)

Geck, Martin (2000) *Von Beethoven bis Mahler*, (Reinbek: Rowohlt)

Magee, Bryan (2002) *Wagner and Philosophy*, (Harmondsworth: Penguin)

Parker, Patricia (1996) *Shakespeare from the Margins: Language, Culture, Context*, (Chicago: University of Chicago Press)

Schleiermacher, F.D.E. (1931) *Vorlesungen über die Ästhetik*, ed. C. Lommatzsch, (Berlin, Leipzig: de Gruyter)

Schleiermacher, F.D.E. (1942) *Friedrich Schleiermachers Dialektik*, ed. Rudolf Odebrecht, (Leipzig: Hinrichs)

Taylor, Charles 'Rorty and Philosophy' in eds. Charles Guignon und David R. Hiley, *Richard Rorty*, (Cambridge: Cambridge University Press 2003)

Wheeler, Samuel C III (2000) *Deconstruction as Analytic Philosophy*, (Stanford: Stanford University Press)

Prolegomena to any Future 'Ethics of Music'

It would be very hard to argue that music has nothing to do with *aesthetics*, and it can be argued that aesthetics in its present-day forms was actually made possible by the development of autonomous music at the end of the eighteenth century. This development freed the understanding of art from the need to relate art to something which legitimated it in extra-artistic terms, be it as a means of conveying religious ideas, of representing the world, or of representing human feelings and moral sentiments, e.g. in music or painting. The initial question here is, then, how the new discipline of aesthetics relates to ethics, given that music moves aesthetics away from a direct link to ethics. Even though his ideas played a role in establishing aesthetic autonomy, Kant still wanted art to be closely linked to the ethical. A key aspect of the *Critique of Judgement* is that 'aesthetic ideas' are a means of making accessible non-empirical ideas about how the world should be, in the form of perceptible symbols. Kant, of course, had little time for music, even though the notion of aesthetic ideas becomes important in Romanticism for the way in which it is linked to music as that which can say what language cannot. In the *Athenäum Fragments*, Friedrich Schlegel already claims in 1798, however, that: 'A philosophy of art in general [*der Poesie überhaupt*] would begin with the independence of the beautiful, with the proposition that it is separate from the true and the moral and should be separate from it and have the same rights as it' (Schlegel 1988 2 p. 129 Fragment 252). The rise of autonomous music, which cannot be said to have much overt representational or directly ethical content, would seem, therefore, to reinforce the notion that a key aspect of modernity is, as Habermas has claimed, the *separation* of the aesthetic from the ethical and the cognitive.

This separation does seem to become manifest in the most controversial works of aesthetic modernism, from those of Baudelaire to the present, which establish a space of exploration and world-disclosure that is not bound to cognitive and ethical norms, and often challenges those norms in ways which can be considered 'amoral' or even 'immoral'. However, if such works were *merely* immoral it would be hard to see why they should be valued as works of art at all. If they *are* valued as works of art, because they reveal the limitations of existing ethical conceptions, and thus enable a more inclusive view of human possibilities and limitations, they can actually be construed as in some respects ethically significant. The apparent amoralism of Samuel Beckett's work may be, as Adorno argued, a better response to the failure of bourgeois morality in the Nazi period than mere humanistic moralism. The failure of that kind of moralism demands a new kind of response which cannot be couched in the old terms. In Germany it was, for example, the appearance of Günter Grass' satirical – and at first sight amoral – *The Tin Drum* in 1959 that really began effective ethical self-examination in German literature, not the humanist works characteristic of the immediate post-War Period, which failed to find ways of responding to the moral enormity of the events of the Nazi period. It should, then, be clear that there is no straightforward relationship between what philosophical ethics may wish to argue and the way aesthetic works and practices play a role in ethical experience and reflection.

However, if one does wish to use resources from philosophical ethics to approach issues in music the problem is that the contemporary philosophical landscape offers such a huge diversity of positions concerning the nature of ethical thinking that the outlook for a plausible position on music and ethics would seem to be rather bleak. There are, admittedly, some apparently easy ways out here: if one adopts an Aristotelian concern with ethics as being about the good life, as opposed to the Kantian tradition of morality as being about duties and rights, music can easily be regarded as an essential part of human flourishing. In the light of the recent reaction to the end of the Taliban rule and of the banning of most music in Afghanistan this position is obviously rather hard to gainsay. The problem is, of course, that the position does not really tell us anything very much about *why* music is part of the good life, or about which music might not be (and whether it then still counts as music). Obviously Nazi martial music is music in some sense, but which exactly? And do we wish to encourage this sort of 'music'? (It is worth remembering here that the Nazis also used a march by Hanns Eisler...) Another tack here would be to question the attempt to make music and ethics into something general about which one could have a philosophical debate. 'Which music in which ethical context?' is surely the issue, not generalisations about aesthetics and ethics. The question would then come down to a more empirically-oriented sociological investigation of how music and ethics related in peoples' lives in particular contexts.

Such an approach is evidently valuable, and it would be invidious to reject it. Even Adorno, who for a long time was suspicious of the kind of empirical research at issue here, came to see this, in a paradigmatic illustration of the dangers in this area. In the essay 'On the Fetish-Character of Music' of 1938 he had argued that asking listeners about their reactions to music would merely reproduce information about the surface manifestations of cultural production, and thus fail to grasp the real nature of music's significance in a society dominated by the culture industry. This significance had instead to be interpreted by detailed analysis of musical works. In 1968, reflecting on his admitted failure in the Princeton Radio Research Project with Paul Lazarsfeld in 1938, which relied on the assumption just outlined, he admits, however, that: 'It is an open question, which can indeed only be answered empirically, whether, to what extent, in what dimensions the social implications revealed in musical content analysis are also grasped by the listeners' (cit. Dahms 1994 p. 252–3). How, then, are we to establish a way into questions of music and ethics, without falling prey to platitudes or failing to take account of the demands for empirical legitimation of any claims we might make?

First let us briefly consider some basic matters. Take these two possible approaches. On the one hand, we might consider the question as follows. If philosophy is divided up into discrete areas like epistemology, ethics, and aesthetics, we may reject any supposed conflation of the differing spheres and seek to establish the nature of each domain via its difference from the others. The alternative, to which I shall return in a moment, is that we will have to question the nature of those divisions. On the other hand, it might seem clear that this question cannot be dealt with until we establish just what uses of the term ethics are involved here. Are we talking about the search for ways of legitimating and judging actions, the search for the content of the good life, the search for ways of making decisions on the maximisation of benefit for the majority? More specifically, are we talking about music as a resource for ethical insight, or as a practice which is part of what constitutes a meaningful life, or as a social good to be weighed in terms of its effects on the well-being of the majority? To be honest, I think the results of this sort of analysis will not get us very far. We are likely to end up with another version of the kind of debate on the status of the musical work (is it the score, this performance, all performances, the 'compliance class' of performances that play all the right notes, etc., etc.?) that paralysed the analytical philosophy of music for too long. Trying to establish the definition of a practice or an entity which may actually resist any useful definition, of the kind sought by those held prisoner by the concept of the 'musical work', has proved to be a mistake in philosophical aesthetics. Indeed, in the present case we are faced with two, as they used to be called, 'essentially contested concepts', music and ethics, neither of which is likely to be given an initial characterisation that will really satisfy anybody. The point is, however, that this may not be such a big problem.

These days it is increasingly clear that 'conceptual analysis', of the kind that seeks some kind of definitive resolution of a conceptual difficulty, simply fails to come to terms with the way in which the use of essential terms like 'music' can only be understood holistically, in relation to a historically shifting series of human practices. In other words, if we do not think of language primarily in terms of representation of pre-given objects and entities, and think of it instead as communicative practice, we may be more likely to address productively what it is that those concerned with an issue like music and ethics are concerned with, instead of trying as philosophers to dictate to them what their concepts should mean. This need not commit us to renouncing some sort of perhaps more attenuated, and historically aware, foundational thinking about morality, or even about music, but should remind us that we cannot rely on establishing firm foundations in order to investigate something which concerns us.

The danger of this suggestion, however, is that one ends up with a merely descriptive, historicist account of how ethics and music have been linked at various times in various locations, from the theological to the operatic. Once again, such an enterprise has its own validity, but at some point judgements have to be made which differentiate between those conceptions which can add to our insight into these questions, and those which are now of solely historical interest. We might seem to be led now to a kind of 'relativism of the contemporary position', where we see everything in terms of the world we happen to inhabit, but a further reflection can help dispel this worry. As I have argued in some detail elsewhere, there has recently been a growing convergence between positions in the area of contemporary pragmatism and the broadly understood German Romantic tradition of philosophy primarily associated with the names Novalis, Schlegel, and Schleiermacher (see Bowie 1997, 2003). This convergence has not least to do with the fact that the more rigid versions of the divisions between the cognitive, the ethical, and the aesthetic are coming to be seen as obstacles to insight into the significance of the interplay between them. The desire for such an interplay is integral to Romantic thinking and had been increasingly lost in the wake of the decline of German Idealism and the rise of 'positivism', in the broad sense of philosophy oriented towards the methods of the natural sciences. In consequence, Schlegel's remark, cited above, should not be read as his definitive statement on the matter. In the remark cited he is clearly concerned to establish aesthetic autonomy at a time when it largely did not exist, because art was subordinated to heteronomous social functions. Schlegel is, though, also insistent, in numerous places in his work, that the failure to consider the interplay between different kinds of human practice can be the source of serious cultural impoverishment.

The aim of much of the contemporary pragmatist revival of the ideas of this tradition – a revival which shows little awareness of its convergence with the Romantic tradition (associating itself more often with Hegel) – is to question the scientistic temper of much philosophy today. It aims to do so without, as some later developments in the Romantic tradition do, denying the legitimate role of the natural sciences, both in the objective characterisation of the nature of the world, and in our self-descriptions. Now consider the following example. In an intriguing passage from the *Gay Science* Nietzsche initially exemplifies an extreme anti-science stance when he claims that natural science may be 'one of the *most stupid*, that is, the poorest in meaning [*sinnärmsten*] of all possible world-interpretations'. His example of why this might be the case is music. A science which relies upon 'how much of [music] can be counted, calculated, brought into formulae' would be absurd: 'What would one have grasped, understood, recognised of it! Nothing, almost nothing, of that which is really "music" in it!...' (Nietzsche 1980 Vol. 3 p. 626). The characteristic hyperbole of the initial remark gives way, then, to something much more significant when Nietzsche specifies what he means. The question now is the following: is Nietzsche's objection to the reduction of music to what science can say about it itself cognitive, ethical, or aesthetic? The cognitive objection is that one has failed successfully to characterise the real object 'music'; the ethical objection is that one is failing to do justice to music as something of human value; the aesthetic objection is in many respects the same as the ethical, though it does not require an answer to the question as to whether this kind of evaluation can really apply to inanimate things, rather than only to people. How is one to characterise the differences between these kinds of judgement, given that they are in many respects saying much the same thing?

If we adhere to the assumption of the separation of the spheres of modernity, in the manner of Habermas, we might try to argue that Nietzsche's objection can be related to three different types of communicative action with differing aims, which demand different kinds of legitimation. The cognitive form of communicative action involves a question – 'Does science grasp music as music?' – that demands a 'Yes/No' answer which is backed up with reasons. The ethical objection would have to be judged in terms of whether the failure appropriately to interpret the nature of music offends against a socially agreed norm. Here the question is whether this evaluation is merely local to a specific life-world, which for certain kinds of philosopher puts it in the realm of what they mean by the 'ethical', or whether it has a stronger normative force that is binding beyond that context, which would link it to the 'moral'.

These reflections give rise to a rather complex issue. While it is arguable that moral judgements are in fact cognitive judgements, and thus open to assessment as to their truth, this is much more controversial with regard to aesthetic judgements, which seem less amenable to consensus of any kind as to their truth, even within specific life-worlds. However, Nietzsche actually has to invoke music's *aesthetic* value in order to ground the judgement that a scientific explanation of music is *false* because it does not tell us what makes a series of sounds into music and thus misses the significance of a vital cultural practice. If this is the case, one can, if one accepts that normativity plays a decisive role in both science and aesthetics, make true judgements about art, which rely on aesthetic grounds that are as valid as those in the sciences. The importance of this kind of claim is that it itself has ethical import because it involves the demand to *do justice* to aspects of the world to which the sciences cannot do justice. What is starting to become apparent here, then, is a sense in which certain kinds of normative issues do not fit neatly into a strict division of the cognitive, the ethical, and the aesthetic.

Now any attempt to arrive at a defensible position here will depend upon the scope of what one terms 'ethical'. Ernst Tugendhat insists on the fact that moral judgements have to be grounded, and tries to illustrate this by contrasting them with aesthetic judgements. Assertions in the moral sphere lay claim to a realm of intersubjective objectivity, such that, even though we may disagree about our conceptions of justice, we cannot but argue, with the hope of a result, about what we think is just. Aesthetic assertions, on the other hand, rely on subjective preferences which can change, and so have no substantial claim to objectivity. (Habermas tends to see the 'ethical' in similar terms to the way Tugendhat sees the aesthetic, restricting the 'moral' to the realm of intersubjective objectivity.) Tugendhat claims that 'A word like "just", which stands for normative fairness between subjects, does not exist in the aesthetic' (Tugendhat 2000 p. 94). At the same time, he argues that without the emotion of indignation, which is the motivational response to the violation of inter-subjectively accepted norms, there can be no way of grounding morality. He admits that there could be the sort of sanction in aesthetic matters which he thinks inseparable from moral judgements based on collectively legitimated norms, but the difference is that in aesthetics there is no necessity for this to be the case, because of the subjective nature of what is at issue.

Much of this seems arguable, but I want to explore certain ways in which Tugendhat's firm line might be made less firm, without thereby abolishing distinctions we should sustain in some form. In a sense what I am doing, then, is deconstructing the distinction. However, as Samuel Wheeler has reminded us, 'Deconstructed distinctions are OK' (Wheeler 2000) – we don't stop using them just because their boundaries are not as firm as they may initially have been taken to be.[3] Tugendhat's choice of the word 'just' points to those words in moral vocabulary which cannot

---

[3] Quine's rejection of the analytic/synthetic distinction should be seen in such terms: the distinction can be useful in certain contexts, even though it may not be a logically necessary distinction.

be reduced to another, non-normative vocabulary, of the kind that was supposed to make ethics based on 'emotivism' – an approach which is thankfully now almost completely discredited. Now the decision as to which words are non-reducible in this manner may be historically and culturally variable, but what matters is the fact that there are words which resist naturalistic reduction, which can therefore be used to make true normative assertions.

The word I want to consider here is the word 'right'. – I should perhaps add at the outset that I do not attribute any great importance to the word itself. – What interests me is how certain kinds of use of the word open up questions for the present discussion. In German 'right' can in certain contexts be translated by 'stimmig', which relates to 'stimmen', to be in tune, and derives from the word for voice. Charles Larmore talks about the idea of 'how we get in tune with the world' (Larmore 1996 p. 9) that cannot be exhausted by the sciences, and the links between rightness and being in tune suggest the direction in which I wish to go. In a moral context, if I say 'It's not right for you to do that', as you are about to push ahead of someone in a queue, this need not be reduced to my not liking what you do, and I can give grounds for my statement that can be connected to some form of social sanction. The use of right in such situations can also, though, be less straightforwardly linked to moral sanction and be more linked to the dissonance such behaviour produces in the social world. 'Right' can, of course, also be used in relation to the solving of a mathematical equation, in which case it seems to have the function of saying that the equation is a true proposition.

But now consider the following. Tugendhat analogises aesthetic judge-ments to judgements about whether a wine is good or not (an example already used by Kant to distinguish between the 'agreeable' and the 'beautiful'). Tugendhat's analogy seems to me evidently not an adequate basis for describing such judgements. (It may not even be adequate to the example of wine: are all such judgements merely subjective or is there a level at which someone's preference for *Liebfraumilch* over a fine white wine could be seen as 'not right', because they so lack the kind of discrimination that allows the world to become a more interesting place?). Far more significant than judgements based on the notion of 'good', as Adorno, Nelson Goodman and others have suggested, are judgements about whether something in a work, a performance of a work, or, indeed, a work itself as a whole, is 'right' or not. These judgements require a justification, of the kind Tugendhat thinks applies only to cognitive and moral claims. The easy way out here is to argue that the judgement of rightness has as its ground a feeling, and the feeling is subjective, so we are back with the glass of wine. If this is not satisfactory – and I don't think it is – then we need to think more carefully about the nature of feeling in the aesthetic domain, and about how it relates to the cognitive and the ethical.

Attention to feeling is, of course, particularly significant in the domain of music. However much musicology may be concerned to analyse and interpret music, the basis of these activities is, at least in part, the affective significance of music, which makes it an object of concern in the first place. As we saw, Tugendhat thinks morality requires a ground in feeling if it is to be motivated at all, and this offers some space, of which he takes little or no account, for questioning the ways we divide ethical and aesthetic judgements.

What is at issue, then, is how divisions are made between ways in which things are evaluated and how this relates to the various ways in which we relate to aspects of the world. If one contends that normativity is inherent in all our practices, questions of degree and appropriateness can take on as important a role as questions asked on the basis of the presumed differences between the cognitive, ethical, and aesthetic spheres. Crucial to this approach is the question of relevance: as Goodman, Putnam and others argue, it is possible to generate an indeterminate amount of trivial truths which make no difference to anything in any science. Similarly one can, in music, for example, count the number of notes in a score, or come up with any number of other silly forms of classification. These classifications are about as 'objective' as you can get, and their very futility is what gives rise to Goodman's argument that rightness may often be more important in many contexts than semantically conceived truth. What I am trying to get at, therefore, is the sense in which the 'subjective' aspect of the aesthetic need not be considered as necessarily deficient in relation to scientific objectivity. Unless one takes the cognitive as the prior norm against which all else is measured, an idea which rests on the assumption that the spheres can be distinguished in terms of just one of them, it seems more apt to examine how differing kinds of practice and communication play a role in the world we inhabit. This approach is not intended simply to level all kinds of judgement into some kind of uniformity, as though they were 'all essentially evaluative' in a trivial sense. The issue is rather the nature of what Brandom calls 'discursive commitments', and the example of music is important in extending the focus of the kind of philosophy which makes practices of legitimation its central concern.

One of the characteristic aspects of this kind of philosophical orientation concerns the issue of truth. In a recent essay Albrecht Wellmer has argued, in certain respects against his own previous conception, that a philosophical concern with the semantic truth of single propositions is inadequate to the way in which we should seek to understand truth.[4] He argues that the 'battle for truth' is concerned with 'the appropriateness of our understanding of the world, of problems, of issues, and of ourselves, or the concepts and connections of concepts which are fundamental to these understandings: intentionality, understanding, meaning, truth, morality, knowledge, justice, justification etc.' (in eds. Wingert and Günther 2001 p. 25). Consequently 'the concept of truth points of its own accord to a normative horizon which always already goes beyond that of an argumentative dispute about the truth of single utterances' (ibid. p. 52). Wellmer therefore insists that 'a "world-disclosing" moment

---

[4] I make the much the same point as Wellmer now makes against Habermas and Rorty against Wellmer in Bowie 1997.

is, at least implicitly, always already included in normal linguistic communication and argumentation' (ibid. p. 49). This is because the realm of what concerns us, which we employ as the background to our understandings of particular arguments that we can take as true or false, is prior to any particular question concerning something's truth or falsity. It is not, though, as it seems to be for Heidegger, that this world-disclosive dimension is immune to criticism. As we become aware of the deficits of the version of this dimension within which we are moving, we can seek ways of extending or changing our horizons. Wellmer thinks philosophy plays an essential role in this kind of criticism, but what he says can also make sense in relation to music, not least because of the ways in which it can suggest the limits both of natural scientific and philosophical explanation.

What Wellmer offers is a way of salvaging the difficult link between art and truth characteristic of some Romantic thinking and of Adorno, Heidegger and Gadamer, by reformulating the issue in terms of the normativity of the cultural horizons within which cognitive, ethical and aesthetic concerns are negotiated. In this perspective the kind of contradictions and dissonances which emerge because we fail to incorporate certain dimensions of articulation into our concern with the rightness of what we think, feel, and do can be revealed in a whole variety of ways. Now Wellmer sees this issue in purely linguistic terms, for the simple reason that legitimation and validity are largely dependent on propositional articulation. However, one of the significances of music in the modern period is precisely that it highlights dimensions of communication which resist verbal articulation whilst still involving issues of rightness.[5]

The ability to arrive at musical 'rightness', be it in the playing of music, or the verbal interpretation of music, relies upon the ability to do things in a 'stimmig' manner, which cannot be definitively formulated in words. The tendency has therefore been to regard this as somehow inherently

---

[5] Wellmer has recently developed related ideas to these in Wellmer 2008.

'subjective' in the manner of Tugendhat, but this is simply false in terms of the actual emergence of aesthetic norms and aesthetic disagreements within real societies: Robert Pippin cites the case of opera, whose norms have an objective status to those engaged in the practice of opera, even though their emergence is not the result of individual intention (Pippin 2008 p. 75). The attempt to get it aesthetically right may not be exactly the same as getting it morally right, but the difference is not the one Tugendhat suggests, because it entails intersubjective negotiation which can result in the same kind of consensus as can result in ethical matters. Stanley Cavell remarks that: 'It is essential in making an aesthetic judgement that at some point we be prepared to say in its support: don't you see, don't you hear, don't you dig? ... Because if you do not see something, without explanation, then there is nothing further to discuss' (Cavell 1976 p. 93). This immediacy of aesthetic understanding, the feeling, particularly associated with music, which motivates the need to become involved in a discussion with no obvious conclusion, offers a route into an exploration of music and ethics. The importance of this exploration lies in its demand to expand our horizons beyond the habitual discourses of legitimation, to find kinds of rightness which will never be explained, of the kind that are evident in the disclosive power of the feelings and other relations to the world evoked by music.

References

Bowie, Andrew (1997) *From Romanticism to Critical Theory. The Philosophy of German Literary Theory*, (London: Routledge)

Bowie, Andrew (2003) *Aesthetics and Subjectivity: from Kant to Nietzsche*, (Manchester: Manchester University Press)

Cavell, Stanley (1976) *Must we mean what we say?*, (Cambridge: Cambridge University Press)

Dahms, Hans-Joachim (1994), *Positivismusstreit: die Auseinandersetzung der Frankfurter Schule mit dem logischen Positivismus, dem amerikanischen Pragmatismus, und dem kritischen Rationalismus*, (Frankfurt: Suhrkamp)

Larmore, Charles (1996) *The Morals of Modernity*, (Cambridge: Cambridge University Press)

Nietzsche, Friedrich (1980) *Sämtliche Werke*. Kritische Studienausgabe in 15 Bänden, ed. Giorgio Colli and Mazzino Montinari, (Munich, Berlin, New York; de Gruyter)

Pippin, Robert (2008) *Hegel's Practical Philosophy: Rational Agency as Ethical Life*, (Cambridge: Cambridge University Press)

Schlegel, Friedrich (1988) *Kritische Schriften und Fragmente 1–6*, (Paderborn: Schöningh)

Tugendhat, Ernst (2001) *Aufsätze 1992–2000*, (Frankfurt: Suhrkamp)

Wellmer, Albrecht (2009) *Versuch über Musik und Sprache*, (Munich: Hanser)

Wheeler, Samuel C III (2000) *Deconstruction as Analytic Philosophy*, (Stanford: Stanford University Press)

Wingert, Lutz; Günther, Klaus, eds. (2001) *Die Öffentlichkeit der Vernunft und die Vernunft der Öffentlichkeit. Festschrift für Jürgen Habermas*, (Frankfurt: Suhrkamp)

Beethoven and Romantic Thought

It is often said that the piano sonatas of Beethoven helped effect a change in the very idea of what music is. How that change should be understood is, though, anything but generally agreed. One of the reasons for the failure properly to grasp the issues involved here lies in the widespread neglect of the fact that Beethoven's career as a composer coincides almost exactly with the flowering of philosophy in Germany between the 1780's and 1830's which is regarded by many, including myself, as second only to the first emergence of philosophy in ancient Greece. However, if I now cite the names of the 'early Romantics' Friedrich Schlegel, Novalis, and of F.W.J. Schelling, all of whose important work begins to emerge around 1795, to back up my assertion, I am aware that the assertion will appear incomprehensible to many people. Even adding the more familiar, non-Romantic names of Immanuel Kant and G.W.F. Hegel to my list may initially only serve to induce a headache in some of my audience. Sir Thomas Beecham famously asserted that the English didn't really like music, but just liked the noise it makes: when it comes to philosophy, and particularly to German philosophy, even the noise is usually too much.

Let us try, though, precisely by seeing how it relates to philosophy, to make some sense of the topic of Beethoven and Romanticism in a manner which might make the noise Beethoven makes more interesting. Take the following remark, written in 1943 by the German philosopher, composer and musicologist Theodor W. Adorno, in the notes for his never completed book on Beethoven: 'That music can only say what is particular to music: this means that word and concept cannot *directly* express music's content, but can only do so indirectly, i.e. as philosophy' (Adorno 1993 p. 31). One of the crucial aspects of what I mean by Romantic thought is its development of 'hermeneutics', the art of understanding texts and works of art via an appropriate understanding of their diverse social, conceptual, and historical contexts. Why, then, should Beethoven, as opposed to the more obvious examples of Schumann, Chopin, or Wagner be considered in relation to the context of Romantic philosophy? Given that Carl Dahlhaus has justifiably talked of an 'inner distance' that exists between Beethoven, and his contemporaries Novalis and Schlegel, my task is to establish how there is also a significant connection between them.

We need here, then, to make some distinctions between ways in which the word 'Romantic' is used. 'Romantic' is, for example, often very vaguely used to refer to a new concern in modernity with the self's relationship to the mysteries of nature; more helpfully, it is used to characterise a musical (and a poetic and visual) style that is distinguished from the 'Classical'; too rarely, it is also used to characterise a central series of developments in modern Western philosophy, which begin with the 'early Romanticism' of Schlegel and Novalis. I shall leave out the first of these uses because it is too diffuse to be usefully discussed in a short space. In terms of artistic style, 'Romantic', as Charles Rosen has shown, is often best employed in relation to the breakdown of 'closed', Classical forms. He suggests this by an example which can serve as a useful metaphor, namely Schumann's ending of the first song of *Dichterliebe* with an unresolved dominant seventh chord. This forces the listener to listen and think beyond the confines of the song itself in a way which does not happen in Beethoven -- although, as Rosen suggests, Beethoven does come quite close to it at the end of '*An die ferne Geliebte*'. The *philosophical* use of the term Romantic *can* and should be related to this breakdown in the sense of the work of art as a completed, self-enclosed 'Classical' totality. It does, though, have wider implications which can illuminate – and be illuminated by – Beethoven's music. This is despite the fact that even those compositions of Beethoven – such as the sonatas Opus 27 'Quasi una fantasia' or the 'Pastoral' sonata – which are often thought, because of their formal experimentation and propensity for surprising changes of mood, to be his most 'Romantic', do not break with classical formal assumptions as radically as Schumann and others do. What really interests me in this respect can, however, only be made clear by delving into the philosophy of the period.

In the *Athenäum Fragments*, a series of literary, philosophical and aesthetic reflections of 1800, Friedrich Schlegel made the following startling assertions, which a hundred years previously would have been incomprehensible, and which echo Beethoven's piano music of exactly the same time:

> Many people find it strange and ridiculous if musicians talk about the thoughts in their compositions; and it can often happen that one sees that they have more thoughts in their music than about it. But those who have a sense for the wonderful affinities of all arts and sciences will at least not look at the matter from the flat point of view of so-called naturalness, according to which music is only supposed to be the language of feeling, they will in fact not find it per se impossible that there is a certain tendency of all pure instrumental music towards philosophy. Must pure instrumental music not create a text for itself? and is the theme in it not as developed, confirmed, varied and contrasted as the object of meditation in a sequence of philosophical ideas? (Schlegel 1988 2 p. 155).

Incidentally, soon after writing this Schlegel wrote a wonderful essay in reply to his critics called 'On Incomprehensibility': you are probably thinking you can see why. Things are, though, perhaps not quite that difficult. Schlegel himself seems to have known relatively little about music, but his philosophical imagination and reliance on friends who did know about music made up for this. His main claim lies in the *denial* that music is only the language of feeling, something which is presumably rather unexpected if one assumes a traditional view of 'Romanticism', and which is more in tune with Beethoven's own avowed dislike of people crying when they heard his music.

Schlegel seeks to validate his claim by his Romantic inversion -- inversion of received ideas, rather than rampant subjectivism, *is* a key characteristic of Romantic thought -- of Enlightenment assumptions about the relationship between language and music. In doing so he builds on a broader change in thinking about language and music that had begun around the 1750's. The fact is that from Saint-Evremond's declaration in 1678 that 'The Musick must be made for the Words, rather than the Words for the Musick' (Saint-Evremond 1930 p. 210), one has moved by the later eighteenth century to claims like J.N. Forkel's assertion in 1778 that music 'begins ... where other languages can no longer reach' (Forkel 1778 p. 66). In his *Literary Notes* Schlegel says of the novel, the '*Roman*': 'The method of the novel is that of instrumental music. In the novel even the characters may be treated as arbitrarily as music treats its theme' (Schlegel 1980 p. 146). Elsewhere he maintains that music is 'the highest of all arts. It is the most general [art]. Every art has musical principles and when it is completed it becomes itself music. This is even true of philosophy' (ibid. p. 151). The underlying point is that forms of order established by the repetition and variation of 'musical thoughts' are seen as intrinsically related to other forms of order in the world, even to the extent of their being the most significant kind of order. It is arguable, as Schlegel suggests of the novel, that the modern notion of 'literature' emerges via this link of writing to musical forms of articulation, which takes writing away from being merely concerned with representing a 'ready-made' world and takes account of the rhythmic and other aspects of texts which are crucial to their revelatory aesthetic effects. The influence of Haydn, Mozart and Beethoven on the thought of the period lies precisely in their demonstration of the potential for new forms of rhythmic, melodic and harmonic order that connect to verbal forms. It is, then, the ways in which music is related to other forms of articulation that matter most for Romantic philosophy.

Now it is well known that, until the eighteenth century, music had been generally regarded either as a reflection of the divine order of the universe, or as the depiction of – rather than the means of arousing – feelings. The change in the status of music and other art, particularly at the end of the eighteenth century, has consequently been seen in terms of the tendency in 'Romanticism' for art to take over the role of theology, as a pseudo-religion based on the newly discovered creative freedom of the subject. There is something in this, but the issue is not that simple. It does not, for example, explain why for the first time *music* came be regarded by Beethoven and the Romantics as perhaps the most important way of making – largely – secular sense of the modern world. My answer to this will, I'm afraid, be rather complex, but I hope you will bear with me.

The vital moves in modern philosophy are inaugurated by Kant's break in 1781 – of which Beethoven seems to have been aware – with the idea that philosophy's task is to reflect the truth of a world whose God-given order is already contained within it. The world cannot be *said* by philosophy to be 'ready-made', with its order already imprinted in it, because what it comes to be known as also depends upon our thinking. We can illustrate Kant's contentions via examples in music, as I shall show in a moment. For the Romantics, in the light of Kant, music (and other art) actually becomes analogous to the world in general – Schlegel will talk of the 'endless play of the world' as 'the work of art which constantly forms itself' (Schlegel 1988 2 p. 206), and Schelling, in his 1802–3 *Philosophy of Art*, talks of music as 'nothing but the heard rhythm and the harmony of the visible universe' (Schelling 1854 I/5. p. 329). This position is perhaps not as odd or silly as it might sound. The 'rhythm' of the universe lies in the fact that for there to be any order in the universe we must be able to make different aspects of it identical, in the way that differing beats of a rhythm require us to link them together for them to be a rhythm at all, rather than random noises. We do much the same, as Kant suggested, in forming concepts.

Take, then, this example, suggested by Carl Dahlhaus. In the first movement of Beethoven's E-flat Sonata Opus 31 Number 3 what initially appears as just an introduction turns out to be the main theme, and other parts of the movement change their role once the following part of the context of the movement is established. Something similar happens in Opus 31 Number 2, where the ambiguity as to what the main theme actually is cannot finally be resolved, which is precisely the point. The same kind of question arises with regard to when the second thematic group of the 'Pastoral' sonata actually begins. The slow movement of Opus 27 Number One, which suddenly re-appears in the Allegro finale, and the last movement of Opus 26, whose mood clashes so strangely with the preceding funeral march, pose similar, though perhaps less complex, questions concerning the significance and role in the whole of one part of the work. It is only at the end of a piece that the role of its main elements can be established, and even then, of course, there is likely to be disagreement as to the interpretation of that role. Such examples illustrate the vital aspect of Kant's arguments in the present context. Because we are able to make such *changes* in how we organise phenomena, by coming to 'see' or 'hear' them as something else, we realise that what we habitually think is just 'out there' independently of ourselves also depends for its intelligibility on what Kant termed 'synthesis', our active linking together of aspects of what we receive from the world.

Perhaps most crucially – and this is the central idea exploited by the Romantics – nothing can be seen simply to contain its own identity within itself: what things come to be apprehended as depends upon their changing relationships to other things. The major new factor in the music of this period, which is most manifest in Beethoven's mode of composition, is the new way in which the elements of a composition *only* gain their significance in relation to the developing movement of the particular whole, because traditional forms and conventions whose significance is already established are either abandoned or their function is transformed. As is well known, the attempt to extract isolated beautiful melodies from some of the greatest works of Beethoven is the swiftest way to make a nonsense of them: think of the essentially empty initial thematic material of the opening of the first movement of the *Eroica* Symphony, before the famous dissonant C# that begins the transformation of that material, or of the 'Waldstein' sonata. The insignificance of the initial material is part of what generates the power of the whole, because so much is produced from so little by the continual addition of new contexts and relationships. The first movement of the B-flat Sonata Opus 22 is a much smaller scale, perhaps more ironic example of this. It is, then, this new sense of the possibilities of establishing a unique dynamic totality in music via the organising activity of thought which accords with central philosophical ideas of the time. In Adorno's phrase about Beethoven: 'the sonata is the [philosophical] system as music' (Adorno 1993 p. 231).

The Romantics realised that perhaps the most vital aspect of Kant's conception of philosophy was the imagination, the source of the ability to change what we see and hear things as. In one obvious sense at least, the imagination must also be part of nature, because it is given to us as part of what <u>we</u> are as natural beings. The imagination can be developed, but it must already be active for this to be possible in the first place. The Romantic claim is that very ability of human beings to establish forms of order in art which are connected to forms in the natural world is the source of central insights concerning our place within things. The further key aspect here are, as the Romantics realised clearly for perhaps the first time, 'natural languages', languages which arise and are given to us in a manner beyond our control. It is here that the connection to Beethoven's music begins really to add up, and this becomes most interesting when one introduces a further aspect of the thought of the time, namely the widespread speculation on the *origin* of language that was occasioned by the questioning of the idea of its divine origin.

The essential problem is that any account of the origin of language has to employ precisely what it is trying to explain – language – in order to describe the state before there was language. In the light of this realisation Schelling asserts in 1809–10 that 'because sound and note only seem to arise in that battle between spirituality and corporeality, music (*Tonkunst*) alone can be the image of ... primeval nature and its movement' (Schelling 1946 I p. 43). Schelling's thought has echoes in actual music that seems to wish to evoke the primal conflict via which things come into being by becoming differentiated from other things, for example in the beginning of the Ninth Symphony and the beginnings of many of Bruckner's symphonies, Wagner's *Ring*, or Mahler's First, Second, Seventh and Ninth Symphonies. The 'battle' in question is evident in the everyday fact that sound is produced by oscillation in space of a resisting material body that is set in motion by something opposed to it. Schelling sees this dynamic relationship between something and nothing – the thing and the space it periodically fills – as the basis of how anything in the world becomes intelligible at all, rather than remaining inertly enclosed within itself. In the same way inert natural material – air, for example – is mobilised in linguistic articulation into the living means of manifesting the world of thought. Schelling, whose early work Beethoven apparently admired, was clearly influenced in these ideas by his friendship with the other Romantics at the end of the eighteenth century, and they all connect these ideas to music. Novalis talks, for example, of the 'strange game of relations between things' that is 'reflected in language', and relates it to language's 'musical spirit'. The link to music in such conceptions lies in the fact that language is not primarily understood as that which establishes or re-presents a fixed world of objects, but instead as an ever-changing network of relationships between elements that functions in the same way as the rest of nature, the elements only gaining an intelligible identity, be it as words or as notes, via those relationships.

Enough philosophy – for a moment at least – these issues *are* accessible in common experience. Take the opening movement of the so-called 'Moonlight' sonata. We can all come up with a variety of characterisations of the piece, and some of these characterisations will reveal things to others that would otherwise have remained hidden for them. However, the very idea that one could exhaustively reveal the piece's meaning clashes with the sense that only the music itself can say what it says: a verbal account can only ever help one hear and understand the music better (or worse) by extending the contexts to which it can be related, not replace it by revealing what it refers to or 'represents'. Music cannot be adequately described by another kind of literal language, because its significance will be lost in the process, much as explaining a joke – the joke is, by the way, a key early Romantic category – kills the joke *qua* joke by attempting to replace the effect of the particular *combination* of elements with an account of those elements which does not employ that combination itself. One can, of course, see these issues both ways round. Music can change what we see in a film or apprehend in a text: at the same time, though, the film or text can change our sense of the import of the music. The underlying point is that, although they can all affect each other, none of these forms of articulation and understanding is finally reducible to the others. What reveals an aspect of the world to us need not share the attributes of what it reveals: Adorno suggests, for example, that Rousseau's idea that music can represent repose by its movement is manifested in the 'Pastoral' sonata's first movement.

Wittgenstein, who was familiar with the work of Novalis, will suggest that 'Understanding a sentence in language is much more related to understanding a theme in music than one thinks' (Wittgenstein 1982 p. 226). Verbal attempts to describe or evoke what happens in music almost invariably have recourse to metaphors, a fact which troubles some musicologists. Why, though, should the analysable aspects of music that can be characterised in referential terms – 'the main theme in the key of C#-minor' etc. – always have to take precedence over what music and metaphors which give access to music can 'make us notice' about moods, time, memories, rhythm, the landscape, or whatever, that literal language cannot? The 'Moonlight' sonata's first movement may actually help bring a certain kind of mood into existence for many people, rather than just being a 'reflection' or 're-presentation' of already familiar melancholy. Clearly such music can only 'work' if we already live in a world where such moods are to some degree familiar and where language is part of how the world is intelligible at all, but the music's specific way of *articulating* a mood is not reducible to what is already familiar. The fact is, of course, that we can often understand a piece better via the playing of a great interpreter than we can via the most sophisticated verbal analysis of the score. Adorno maintains in this respect that 'Music can speak via its distance from language and its proximity to language' (Adorno 1993 p. 54), and it is this shifting relationship that is a vital part of Romantic thought and of its relationship to Beethoven's music.

Thus far I have signally avoided trying to answer the apparently obvious question 'Is Beethoven a Romantic?', but, in concluding, I ought to have a go. In a review of the Opus 70 Piano trios in 1813 E.T.A Hoffmann avers that 'Beethoven is more of a purely romantic composer than anyone ever was' (Hoffmann 1988 p. 119), and in the celebrated review of the Fifth Symphony he says that Beethoven's music 'awakes that endless longing which is the essence of Romanticism' (ibid. p. 25). The longing he alludes to is for 'the infinite', and here we do have a clear link of music to Schlegel and the issue of Romantic philosophy. Schlegel famously asserts that '*The essence of philosophy consists in the longing for the infinite*' (Schlegel 1988 5 p. 99). The simple point is that wordless music resists attempts to fix its significance, a fact evident in the endless metaphors one can generate by trying to evoke it in words. Music is therefore seen as able in some way to 'say the unsayable': it remains revelatory in a way that the habitual use of everyday language cannot be. I will come back to this in a moment. The remarks of Hoffmann and Schlegel are, though, further complicated both by the fact that Hoffmann includes Mozart and Haydn among his 'Romantics', and that he and Schlegel insist on a certain kind of reflective sobriety as an essential part of Romanticism, which is then demonstrated in Hoffmann's own acute technical analysis of the Fifth symphony. Clearly the name 'Romantic' does not help very much, once these sorts of divergence emerge. What, though, of 'the infinite', which is an inescapable aspect of Romantic thought?

Talk of the infinite is usually another invitation to vagueness. However, there are specific ways of discussing the infinite which were very much a part of the Romantic thought of this period. If, as we saw, the initial musical material of the beginning of the *Eroica* is lacking and needs what follows it to become significant, it can be said to be 'finite' in a negative sense. When what is initially 'finite' is related to what succeeds it, it becomes drawn into a process which includes it within a whole that gives it its significance, thereby at least partially overcoming its finitude. In this sense the infinite is manifested in the fact that finite things cannot be understood in isolation. Such infinities are the bread and butter of geometry, for example, and are thoroughly determinable by mathematical functions. This sense of a self-contained infinity is, via the influence of Spinoza, the basic thought of Hegel's Idealist system of philosophy, which Adorno insists is vitally related to Beethoven, or at least – and here we come to the heart of the matter – to the 'Classical' Beethoven. What, then, of the 'Romantic' Beethoven?

Adorno claims that: 'One can show via the 1st movement of op. 27 Number 2 how Beethoven, to put it in Hegelian terms, has the whole of Romanticism – not just its "mood" but its form-world – within him, in order to negate it' (Adorno 1993 p. 52). Having shown 'how it can be done', via the use of song form, harmonic ambiguity, and a deliberate lack of contrast in the name of sustaining the underlying mood, Beethoven moves in the 'middle period' to other 'Classical' possibilities, generally leaving this form-world – and its weaknesses – to the Romantics. For Adorno 'Romantic' music gives the particular detail, the 'tune' in Schubert's songs or Impromptus, for example, a subjective expressive value in itself, thereby creating the kind of formal difficulty most evident, say, in the meandering, sequenced development sections of some of Schumann's later works. Beethoven is aware of the possibility of privileging such subjective expressive moments, as the 'Moonlight' Sonata and aspects, say, of Opus 26 demonstrate, but he resists it more often than not, in favour of the negation of the particular 'finite' moment we considered a moment ago. As such, what Adorno terms Beethoven's 'apparent asceticism in relation to the subjective spontaneity of the inspired idea' (ibid. p. 69) is part of an impulse towards the transcending of merely subjective expression that is achieved in the *Eroica*.

However, this move, which echoes Hegel's Idealist conception – the

Eroica and Hegel's first mature presentations of his philosophy are almost exactly contemporaneous – also involves the bringing together of the whole movement by the sonata reprise, in which the formally decisive part of the end of the movement is merely a conventionally determined repetition of the material of the beginning. Hegel regards the revelation of the identity of the beginning with the end as the task of a philosophical system. The philosopher resolves the problem of how thought relates to the world by showing at the end of the system that any initially 'finite' aspect of thought becomes 'infinite', in the sense intended here, when its place in the dynamic whole finally emerges via the philosophical system's ability to determine that place. In this way Hegel thinks he can establish a firm basis for modern philosophy that leaves nothing in principle unsayable (including the significance of music): anything we do not understand is simply a finite contradiction which is overcome by the resolution of that contradiction, which generates further contradictions until the ultimate contradiction between thought and the real is itself overcome. Though the *Eroica* provides a structurally related model of this, it is, Adorno argues, only carried out in the form of 'appearance', as art, because the new freedom to organise musical material into a totality does not carry over into the ability to organise the social and natural world in the same way. The organising power of rational thinking is therefore both manifested and questioned in such music; furthermore, Beethoven himself increasingly moves away from this mode of composition.

The crucial difference between Hegel and the Romantics is that the early Romantics see systematic philosophy as both necessary and condemned to failure. This is what Schlegel meant by philosophy's 'longing': a sense of lack can only be occasioned by some sense of the completion that would overcome that lack – which would make the whole thing add up – but for the Romantics this completion cannot be said to be realisable. Their resistance to the Idealist position is part of what leads them to their concern with music, and thence to the links of music to 'irony', which is manifested in a desire to negate any claim to be able to state an ultimate truth; to 'wit' or 'joke', the result of spontaneous and random combinations of disparate elements; to the 'fragment', the refusal to accept that the parts can be shown to make a final whole; to 'allegory', where what is directly stated or presented is not what is meant, and to the inherent transience of all attempts to grasp the truth. In this respect there are serious reasons to link the most convincing and still living aspects of early Romantic philosophy with the *later* Beethoven, where irony, wit, fragmentariness, allegorical use of, for example, conventional dance and march forms, and problematic temporality are so clearly part of his music. Whereas the Classical Beethoven offers models of how the world can be organised via the power of thought, the late Beethoven suspects any such move towards a final sense of completion, whilst still pursuing the need for a new kind of coherence that includes the most recalcitrant musical material.

The answer to the question of Beethoven and Romanticism, then, like all such answers, comes down in one sense to 'what do you mean?'. Depending on what one defines as Romantic, Beethoven can be said to be it or not, or be it at one time, not at another. A more promising answer would seem to me to be that an exploration of largely forgotten Romantic philosophical ideas in relation to Beethoven may make us understand his musical ideas differently, and vice versa. This answer involves the most characteristic philosophical assumption of early Romanticism, namely the assumption of the continuing insufficiency even of our best attempts to understand, an insufficiency which at the same time gives rise to our continuing desire to find new contexts for seeing both the world and art in a new light.

References

Adorno, T.W. (1993) *Beethoven: Philosophie der Musik*, (Frankfurt: Suhrkamp)

Forkel, J.N. (1778) *Musikalisch-kritische Bibliothek*, (Gotha: Ettinger)

Hoffmann, E.T.A, (1988) *Schriften zur Musik. Singspiele*, (Berlin, Weimar: Aufbau Verlag)

Saint-Evremond, Charles Marguetel de Saint Denis (1930) *The Letters of Saint Evremond*, (London: Routledge)

Schelling, F.W.J. (1946) *Die Weltalter*, (Munich: Biederstein)

Friedrich Wilhelm Joseph Schelling's *Sämmtliche Werke*, ed. K.F.A. Schelling, I Abtheilung Vols. 1–10, II Abtheilung Bde. 1–4, Stuttgart, 1856-61

Schlegel, Friedrich (1980) *Literarische Notizen 1797–1807*, ed. Hans Eichner, (Frankfurt, Berlin, Vienna: Ullstein)

Schlegel, Friedrich (1988) *Kritische Schriften und Fragmente 1—6*, (Paderborn: Schöningh)

Wittgenstein, Ludwig (1982) *Philosophische Untersuchungen*, (Oxford: Blackwell)

Background capabilities and prereflexive awareness: the case of improvisation[6]

The introduction of a jazz syllabus by the Associated Board of the Royal Schools of Music led to one of those characteristically uninformative debates in the media about whether improvisation can be taught. The debate was unlikely to get very far because it was never made clear just what anyone thought jazz improvisation really consisted in, the assumption being that it is wholly different from playing music in a non-improvised manner, of the kind that can be taught, at least to some people. My first reaction was to think of one of the oldest, still endlessly disputed questions in philosophy, namely whether 'virtue' can be taught. As with all philosophical problems of this kind, the point of the question is supposed by many to lie in seeking a positive or negative answer, even though the rest of the non-philosophers carry on trying, or not, to make their kids behave, or trying to do the right thing at work without going too much against their principles, which tend to be based on 'do as you would be done by'. None of this, of course, produces a clear answer to the question of what 'virtue' means: it certainly does not, for example, now mean what it did to Plato and Aristotle. The fact that one can't wait for the answer from the philosophers before doing what one has to do anyway has, via the influence of the hermeneutic tradition – the tradition which thinks that scientific explanations are just one way we have of coping with the world – and Wittgenstein, begun to force some philosophers to take a different view of just what it is that they are doing. I hope, therefore, that nobody expects me to give an account of whether, on the basis of the theories I shall be discussing, one can really teach

---

[6] The first version of this paper was given at the Royal Academy of Music in London

improvisation. The fact is that the relationship between theory and praxis in philosophy has always caused trouble, and no doubt will continue to do so, but that need not be the exclusive focus of anyone looking for better ways of reflecting on the question of improvisation.

On the other hand, I do think there is some value in discursively exploring the ways in which we think we are carrying out our practices, even if there is a growing sense in the kind of philosophy I advocate that this reflection is, as Richard Rorty has suggested, just another part of the praxis itself, rather than being the 'philosophy of improvisation', or the 'philosophy of music', or whatever. So how might one approach this issue, which has, it must be said until recently (and this is significant) hardly formed a major focus of philosophical reflection? When one embarks on an improvisation, it is clear that one somehow knows what one is doing, if one has either has been well taught or if one has simply found it quite easy to imitate the sort of thing other people seem to be doing when the word 'improvise' is used to describe what they do. At the same time, nearly everyone has a feeling – despite, or even because of Thelonious Monk's famous injunction that 'Wrong's right' – that one can get it wrong, and the more one knows and plays, the more this feeling tends to grow. Getting it wrong would initially seem to depend upon the failure to follow some kind of rule. When, for example, one writes a sentence without a main verb in a text that is supposed to be setting out a clear case, there is a pretty universal sense that this is breaking the kind of rule which constitutes part of the very practice of appropriate argument. This does not just apply to highly formalised activities. It may be the case that free jazz abolishes one kind of bum note, but it is also the case that the consistent attempt within a free jazz group to play tonally and within a song structure against what the others are doing (which can admittedly be a good idea some of the time in free jazz) itself begins to count as doing it wrong.

It might seem, then, that the meaningfulness of these practices depends upon the correct following of their particular rules, rules which we often seem to be able to specify. Assuming one has got sufficiently advanced technology, it would therefore also seem that a well-programmed computer could do the sort of thing free jazzers do, by giving it the right kind of rules and adding the right degree of randomisation. Now this sort of thing begins to make some people uneasy: surely what counts are the sympathetic vibes between the members of a group, and their own particular talents for innovation? But if those talents can only be realised by remaining within the rules of the practice in question, this would seem to mean that the idea of the creative, 'Romantic' self begins to dissolve into the idea of a rule-following mechanism with a randomised element. I am aware that this crude opposition is not adequate to either position, but the contrast seems heuristically useful. So what can philosophy tell us about such views of the nature of improvisation?

One of the ways I think philosophy can still usefully be done is to look at the history of reflection on an issue and trace how it has filtered into other discussions. This changes the perspective on what one is trying to understand by re-contextualising it, thus creating connections to ways of thinking that are often not part of existing discussion. Most philosophers in this country think the originator of the main discussions of rule-following was Wittgenstein. However, the crucial insight that informs Wittgenstein's ideas was actually arrived at by Kant and some of his contemporaries in the 1780s and 1790s, and they arrived at it not least by thinking about art. The insight is the following: if one assumes that what one does in most situations – including when improvising a jazz solo – is to follow some kind of rules, one is faced with the following dilemma in explaining this idea. What rule does one follow to determine which rules one is to follow? Moreover, what rule did one follow when one learned the first rule one ever learned? Was it the rule for learning rules, and if it was, how do we know that without already presupposing knowledge of what a rule is, thereby ending in a circle? Kant actually defines concepts as rules for identifying objects, including, one presumes, rules themselves. (Note for the philosophers: Kant says, though, that the most basic functions of judgement, the rules according to which we judge whether something is one or many, etc. – the categories – 'cannot be defined without circularity, because the definition would itself have to be a judgement and therefore would already have to contain these functions' (*Critique of Pure Reason* p. A 245).) If all there is to it were rules, one would end up with a regress of rules for choosing rules that has to come to a halt somewhere if one is to do or think anything intelligible at all. Kant therefore suggested that what made judgement – for which we can substitute 'intelligible activity', on the grounds that playing jazz might be seen in part as making a series of very rapid judgements – possible was an 'art hidden in the depths of the human soul', which we are unlikely finally to fathom, namely the art required to explain why there is no regress of rules. The way Kant puts this might seem to take us into the realm of deepest Romantic speculation, and in some senses I think it does, but one first needs to be clearer about just what is being said.

Kant is evidently referring to something which is fundamental to the I, namely the ability to apply rules correctly, which cannot be explained by rules themselves. He famously divides the nature of the mind into an aspect which is passive, or, as he puts it, 'receptive', and an aspect which is active, which he terms 'spontaneous'. The 'art' in question therefore has something to do with 'spontaneity', which refers to what is 'cause of itself', and so does not depend on being caused by something else. In the rationalist philosophy of the seventeenth and earlier eighteenth centuries which Kant did much to invalidate, God was regarded, for example by Spinoza, as 'cause of Himself'. What Kant seems to be suggesting – and this is certainly how he was understood by the more excitable of his successors like the early Fichte – is that the subject is, at the most fundamental level, the cause of its own activity. While it is clear to Kant that our bodily nature is dependent on the same laws as the rest of nature, our ability to countermand naturally caused inclination in the name of what we think we ought to do seems to derive precisely from a source which cannot be bound by laws in the same way. Importantly, Kant's arguments imply that even rule-bound knowledge requires the art in question, because, without the ability to judge in a non rule-bound way what is relevant in the world for what one wants to know, one gets into the regress of judgements. (This problem is, by the way, as Hubert Dreyfus has suggested, the one which shows why certain conceptions of 'artificial intelligence' are bound to fail: by adding more and more rules to cope with the required 'background knowledge' for establishing relevance, one makes the activity which we humans simply do without even thinking more and more complex.)

We don't need to get into the complexities of this issue to summarise the crucial insight for our topic, an insight which was best developed by the theologian and philosopher, F.D.E. Schleiermacher in the early 1800s, namely that 'art' in Kant's sense is any activity in which the application of the activity is not given with the rules for the activity. What, then, does this mean for an account of improvisation? The advantage of Schleiermacher's conception is that, because it assumes a degree of activity on the part of the subject even where one might assume the subject is merely following mechanical rules, it avoids the idea of an inexplicable switch from activity to passivity within the same self. Which bit of the self actively decides that it itself is going to be passive? How does something passive actively cease to be passive? Even our passive ways of being are therefore not merely passive. The real question is the degree to which an activity is rule-bound, which can vary from a great deal, in what is merely habitual, to much less, when the rules just provide the parameters within which one can count as doing the activity at all. One informative example of this (the example is Schleiermacher's) is the difference between a conversation about the weather, and a conversation in which two people come to a new understanding of their relationship by redefining the ways in which they are able to talk about each other.

This latter case brings us closer to the situation of playing jazz, or other kinds of collective improvisation. Let's, then, look at a bit more of the 'phenomenology' of a conversation, much of which seems to me to inform what goes on in improvisation. When communication 'works' each person in the conversation says what they say without 'thinking it up in their head' before they say it. The sort of communication where one formulates most of the words in inner speech before externalising them is a special case, probably known best to the lawyers of President Clinton. Even in this case the sort of thing that can meaningfully be said next seems to emerge as a matter of course, because the previous speaker's utterance partially determines it. One seems to speak into a space which already gives initial shape to what it is that one has to say. This situation has best been described by the German philosopher, Hans-Georg Gadamer, who insists on the 'dialogical' nature of thinking and talking, arguing that one is not an isolated mind that uses words, but rather that in thinking and talking one is always oriented to others in a 'tradition' which is itself a kind of conversation. This is, of course, another way of talking about the sort of thing Wittgenstein sees in terms of the rules underlying our everyday practices, rules, of course, of which we need not consciously be aware. The role of tradition in improvisation is, of course, essential: how otherwise are players who do not know each other able to play together successfully?

We might seem now to be drifting towards aspects of the 'mechanical' account I gave earlier, because tradition can seem merely rule-bound, so we need to ponder the exact nature of novelty in improvisation, as well as ponder certain differences between conversation and the playing of music. Improvisation in conversation seems in one sense to be ubiquitous: there is never an absolutely binding rule which determines what one has to say next, even though there are plenty of situations where the particular communicative practice demands one say something already established in advance, for example in a play, or during a mass, or, for that matter, under extreme – or even relative – coercion. At the same time, it does not seem right to call what one is doing in everyday communication improvising. This may be because the kind of novelty involved requires no particular skill and is not thematised in the activity itself (an issue best explored in Kafka's wonderful story about aesthetics, 'Josephine, the Singer, or the Mouse People'). When it comes to literature it is, at least in the modern period, often the case that novelty is what defines 'the literary', because existing possibilities of speaking or writing are extended. Schleiermacher argues that this 'literary' ability can come into play even in everyday conversation, though it largely does not. One easy way of making it do so is to construct random metaphors, by saying x is y when the two may never been linked together before. If this 'works' – and we have no firm rules for saying when it will, though some metaphors clearly work where others do not – we can have what the German Romantics call 'wit', a transient illumination that results from the success of a new combination. Something similar seems to have been the case in the history of jazz improvisation, for example in the working out of the use of the flat fifth/sharp eleventh and flat ninth, which entailed 'wrong' combinations until people realised they could be used in contexts where they had previously been avoided.

The question is what exactly it is that extends linguistic and musical usage in this way, by transcending existing usage? Despite his attention to poetry Wittgenstein has nothing much to say about this. The analogy to music can, though, be informative here: in both language and music what happens in innovation is rarely the invention of something wholly new – even sound poems made up of previously non-existent words are not particularly startling in this respect, though they do seem to be a largely modern phenomenon – what is happening is rather that reasonably determinate elements are being organised in novel ways. Now it is well known that computers can do this, so novel organisation alone is not what is at issue, but rather novel organisation which is understood by listeners as being meaningful because the elements 'work' together, are somehow 'right'. German calls this 'stimmig', which relates to 'getting in tune', 'stimmen', and this seems a crucial aspect of what I am interested in here because we rely on differing kinds of this phenomenon for most successful aspects of life where we do not just rely on doing what we have always done.

In linguistic innovation there is a sense in which what one says is 'meaningless', if one assumes meaning is fully established via the existing socially-agreed rules which enable something to be comprehensible. These rules are often defined in terms of the recipient of the utterance knowing when it would be true to make the utterance, in terms of what philosophers call 'truth conditions'. In music, though, nothing can be said to be meaningful in this sense, because music does not represent 'states of affairs', or whatever, even if it can say things like 'it's time to get up'. However, this is contentious territory; the borderline may not be quite as clear as this. If one agrees, for example, that, as the philosopher of language Donald Davidson says, 'meaningless' new metaphors can make us notice things that might otherwise remain concealed, one might want to say that music can make us notice things in a related manner, most obviously about things like moods. One would not, note, think that it would be meaningful to talk about the music's 'truth' in the 'propositional' sense just mentioned, though one might very well talk about its 'rightness', its 'Stimmigkeit'. But what role does the producer of the new articulation play in all this?

The odd, and important thing is that what gives rise to novelty does not appear in the world at all – hence the temptation to make it analogous to the random functioning of a system like a computer. What does appear in the explicable object world is the configuration of a series of material phenomena by something that emits or produces them in some other way. As such, the subject 'appears' only in the spaces which make the phenomena – be they words or notes – into something significant, not in the elements which are configured. The philosopher Schelling, a successor of Kant, offers a potentially illuminating metaphor here. Schelling argued that nature's constant cycles of death and regeneration mean that what is essential about nature is 'productivity', not its 'products', the transient phenomena of the natural world. The crucial point for Schelling is that the productivity cannot itself appear, because by doing so it would cease to be itself and become a product.

If we allow that the subject is somehow active in configuring words and notes, it seems to be akin to this productivity, because our only access to it is via its products, which, qua products, are made of the same relatively inert stuff as everything else. The significance of the products is therefore not given in their objective appearance and requires other subjects for it to be appreciated at all. In this view the pleasure and insight afforded by improvisation would lie in our apprehending the productivity which we feel in our own ability for spontaneous innovation through the moving organisation of musical material. Much the same conception is, one should note, necessary to any apprehension of a material manifestation as art, rather than as a mere object. However, it is the non-representational art of music which seems best able to evoke the aspect of the self which resists objectification, and it is significant that the self becomes the central focus of philosophy at the end of the eighteenth century when music without words is elevated by many thinkers into being the highest art, from being – as it still was, at least in some respects, for Kant – one of the lowest. It does, then, seem appropriate in some sense to talk about improvisation in relation to the freedom of the self, though this freedom needs to be understood in the perhaps somewhat negative and limited terms I have suggested. Rather than some kind of original creativity, it is the non-appearing instance which can reconfigure what appears in new ways.

This perhaps rather abstract account might be useful in considering the vexed question of the phenomenology of improvisation. I'll talk about myself for a moment. Quite a lot of the time I have, when playing, stock material which I know I can use over certain chord sequences, though I often decide deliberately not to use it, in a sort of endeavour to try to be productive, rather than just relying on existing 'products'. A vital aspect of my experience corresponds to the phenomenology of language use: I have only the vaguest sense in advance of what I am about to play, at the very most a few bars, and I rarely think of the names of the notes, just the pattern of movements they involve which are a kind of anticipatory frame that can be adjusted in the light of what is going on around me. On my rare good nights I seem able to improvise cogently with only minimal reflective awareness of what I am playing. I suspect other people, especially those better trained than I, may well experience this somewhat differently, but this is a psychological point which does not necessarily affect the more basic issue. The philosophical question is 'where does the novel stuff come from?', given that quite a lot of it just seems to happen, rather than be intended in the sense that many even fairly instinctive actions can be said to be intended. Now it is pretty clear to me that what little people play that is really innovative still largely relies on varying material that has been learned mechanically in practising. However, even though most of what most people play is not very interesting, because it is the result of past practice or, in my case, ineptitude, there do seem to be moments when something different emerges in a way one cannot control because one is not conscious in that way in the first place when playing. The interesting philosophical issue is this strange sense that what produces the improvisation resists objectification: the products, sequences of notes, are much like everyone else's (though virtually never exactly the same), and they are usually nearly within the acknowledged rules – think of the history of jazz styles and the changes in the canon of the permissible – but the production of the products does not seem describable in the kind of terms we use for mechanisms. They seem to have a kind of 'unconscious' intention which transcends what we can control which is not simply reducible to the sum of prior training, not least because it also results dialogically, in the manner of the conversation I talked about earlier.

One way of trying to get a handle on all this is to think in terms of what Kant and others called 'schematism', which he sees as necessary for avoiding the rules for rules regress, namely a function of our thinking and acting (for Kant thinking is a kind of action) which makes things initially intelligible and gives them a form without them having to be fully conceptualised. Not just improvisation but the very ability to produce music and hear it as music seems to rely on something like this, for Kant, ultimately inexplicable 'rule-governed spontaneity', as David Bell has termed it. In music schematism functions without rigidifying into finally specifiable rules. Schematism is therefore both what helps us establish identities between different phenomena, which we do in learning repeatable rules (and thus in cognition), and what may enable us to innovate. The fact is that without this capacity to apprehend and establish identities there would be no sense in which repetition or rhythm (which Schelling termed the 'music in music') would come to be significant at all, and innovation with established material would remain fixed by the rules governing that material. Does this, then, provide an explanation of improvisation and the I? It is here that philosophical ways very often part. One fraction looks to come up with a verifiable explanation of what is at issue which will fit in with explanations of the rest of the world in science. The other fraction maintains that explanations do not extend this far, because what is doing the explaining is trying to explain its own ability to come up with explanations, and this relies on an understanding of what explanation *is* which cannot be explained without moving in a circle. As a member of the latter camp, I think this leads to an important cultural issue, which has political and other implications for how we value our differing kinds of practices. The fact is that the desire to get to an explanation of what happens in real innovation of the kind which we value in the history of music misses the aesthetic point. It is precisely the new articulation which adds *of its own accord* to the world's meaningfulness, without needing to be explained, which is why we continually look for new ways of doing things, including by improvisation. Productivity, one might say, makes life valuable, mere products can end up removing this kind of value. While it is vital that we gain appropriate kinds of understanding of music and its significance in relation to the self, which will reveal more and more of what is significant about music for human beings and enable them to take part in it, a final explanation of the self's relation to music would need to objectify both as mere 'products'. I think there are more than sentimental reasons for resisting this approach to the world.

Shakespeare, Tragedy, and the Philosophical Discourse of Modernity

In his *Philosophy of Art* Schelling complains about English commentators on and admirers of Shakespeare who 'always attend to particular representations of passion, of a character, to psychology, to scenes, to words, without any sense for the whole and for art. If one casts a glance at English commentators, Tieck says very aptly, it is as if, travelling in a beautiful district, one drives past a tavern in front of which drunken peasants are having a row' (Schelling 1/5 p. 725). The answer to the English empiricists would seem, then, to be a good dose of German philosophy. However, here the question arises as to whether philosophy can really tell us about Shakespeare, or whether it should be it vice versa. This perhaps rather crude question begins to look a bit less crude when we ponder the ways in which some recent literary theory has dealt with major literary texts. There has been a tendency in much literary theory for a pre-conceived theory just to dictate how the text can be approached. Characteristic approaches for this kind of theory with regard to Shakespeare involve, for example, looking, in the wake of Foucault and others, at what has been repressed by dominant discourses, particularly with regard to race and gender, or seeking out the ever more specific historical factors which are seen as constituting 'Shakespeare'.

I certainly don't want to deny that these approaches have led to significant insights, which help to render readers more aware both of blind-spots in their apprehension of cultural products and of the often neglected contingencies of history's impact on culture. Neither do I wish to advocate a view which claims that one can approach a text without prejudice, thus avoiding the supposed 'theoreticist' trap by somehow reading in a manner not informed by pre-judgements concerning what is significant. Clearly 'prejudice', in the general sense of background knowledge, as Gadamer has shown, informs all cultural judgement. We can't step outside of and question at one go all our assumptions that enable us to cope in the world. This means there is no neutral place to go in our critical assessments of culture, though we can still be self-reflexively critical with respect to particular issues. However, what sometimes seems to be missing in certain versions of literary theory is a sense that theories might learn from the texts which they are used to interrogate. (This is, incidentally, even more the case for the analytical philosophy of art.) It is one of the great strengths of the work of Stanley Cavell that he seeks ways to learn from the texts with which he engages. He says of his work on Shakespeare and scepticism, for example, that 'The misunderstanding of my attitude that most concerned me was to take my project as the application of some philosophically independent problem of scepticism to a fragmentary parade of Shakespeare's texts' (Cavell 2003 p. 1). I want here to look at a few ramifications of the issue of Shakespeare and philosophy in relation to some modern philosophical responses to the idea of tragedy, and this will form a kind of prolegomenon to what one might say in more detail in this respect about Shakespeare's texts. In the face of an audience, the vast majority of whom certainly know far more about Shakespeare than I do, it seems more sensible for me to tell you what I know something about, that might shed some different light on what I don't know enough about.

In discussion of tragedy from a modern philosophical perspective, one frequent assumption about the history of tragedy is that tragedy was replaced by philosophy as the dominant form of self-understanding in Greek culture, and that this is part of a more general move towards forms of rationality based on the elimination of myth as the dominant form of explanatory response to the world. This story about tragedy was put in question by Nietzsche in the *Birth of Tragedy*, which suggested that tragedy's demise involved the loss of essential insights into the nature of existence that were covered up by 'Socratic optimism' based on the advance of scientific knowledge of the workings of nature. Nietzsche made this suggestion while proposing that the work of Wagner was the contemporary manifestation of a revival of myth and tragedy. The fact that the form of tragedy he was advocating involved music as a core component will become important later in what I have to say. One can, however, ask, as Nietzsche himself came to do, whether in this text he was not just substituting a Schopenhauerian pessimism for Enlightenment optimism, so replacing one questionable philosophical appropriation of tragedy with another, rather than really seeing what tragedy communicates that philosophy might not. This ambiguity with regard to the understanding of tragedy can lead us to a series of interesting issues concerning modern philosophy's relationship to tragedy, not least – and this will be my main topic – in the form of questions about the relationship between Greek tragedy and modern tragedy, which some important, though sometimes neglected, philosophers associate precisely with Shakespeare.

It should already be remembered here that the relationship between philosophy and tragedy can, as Cavell suggests, be seen the other way round from the one just touched on. Indeed, it may well be that there can be no strict boundary between the two if one is not to prejudge too many issues that are vital to human self-understanding. If we can learn things from tragedy which touch on central concerns of human life that cannot be as effectively conveyed by philosophical argument and explanation, tragedy takes on the status of a kind of philosophy. My claims in this respect will be similar to those of Cavell, but will in the main derive from different sources. The fact is that significant ideas in German Idealism, for example, seem themselves to have been generated by the new understanding of Greek tragedy that begins to develop in the second half of the eighteenth century. Hölderlin, Schelling, and Hegel were all concerned with the significance of tragedy from early in their careers. In varying ways all these figures became concerned with Hegel's idea of the 'identity of identity and difference'. In a text from his later period Schelling sums up one way of understanding this idea, when he says that the 'oldest Greek tragedy' reveals that 'it is the mourning/tragedy ('*Trauer*') of everything finite that in itself it is the same as the infinite, but not to *be* the infinite, but rather *not* to be it. It is only to be in *potentia*' (Schelling 1969 p. 90).

Schelling's remark needs a bit of explaining. On one level it is simply a statement of our awareness of finitude. This troubles us because thought seems to take us beyond the finite: it generates the capacity to mourn the lack inherent in all transient, finite things. – The later Nietzsche might be seen as trying to overcome the temptation of thought to seek the infinite in things which will pass away, though he does not seem to offer an alternative that really deals with the reasons for the power of the temptation. – Schelling elsewhere talks in relation to the sense of finitude in all particular things of a 'veil of melancholy which is spread over the whole of nature, the deep, indestructible melancholy of all life' (Schelling 1/7 p. 399). Questions about the nature of finitude can be formulated in other ways, not least in terms of the structures encountered in tragedy. The idea of the identity of identity and difference can be interpreted via the example of Oedipus. He, as the same person, is both father of his daughters and their brother, son of and husband of his mother, detective and the criminal whom the detective is seeking, saviour of the city and the source of the threat to the city. These contradictory roles cannot be sustained by a human individual, who is a relative, 'finite', part of 'the infinite', even though reality as a whole, 'the infinite' itself, can produce a being in whom they are embodied. The human being is brought down by the contradictory nature of being both limited in insight and yet aware of the demand that one be responsible for what one cannot concretely have known, which would require super-human insight. Oedipus only gains full insight at the moment when he is compelled by judgement of his actions to blind himself, thus, of course, embodying a further case of a unity of opposites in the same person.

Such an interpretation suggests how an essential aspect of Greek tragedy played a role in Hegel's thought. A major concern of German

Idealism is with how the One and the Many relate, and with how to come to terms with the fact that the same thing can appear at different times in ways which seem to contradict each other. This gives rise to the idea of a One – the absolute, the infinite – whose essence is the endless creation and destruction of particularity, and the idea is associated with the idea of Dionysus, the God of tragedy, who is torn apart and reborn. Hölderlin in particular will associate Dionysus with the idea of the Christian passion from which a new life emerges, and German Idealism uses this link to argue that contradiction can be resolved into a higher harmony. Hegel refers explicitly to the idea of the Dionysian in the *Phenomenology of Mind*, when he says that 'the true' is the 'Bacchic frenzy in which no member is not drunk; and, because each, as it separates itself, just as immediately dissolves itself, the frenzy is equally transparent and simple tranquillity' (Hegel 1970 p. 47).

Tragedy thus becomes a source of the idea that all particularity is necessarily eventually negated. Importantly, tragedy itself is then in turn interpreted in terms of the philosophical idea. The detailing of the differing ways in which particulars relate to a whole in which they are comprehended is the basis of Hegel's system, and the kinds of relation in question occur at all levels of his system. Hegel says in the *Lectures on the Philosophy of Art* of 1823, for example, that 'In the tragic it is above all that individuality is destroyed by the one-sidedness of its purpose. Individuality with its purpose is destroyed' (Hegel 2003 p. 301). It is destroyed by what Hegel terms 'the eternally substantial' (ibid.), the law of the community, which restores a higher harmony via the result of the conflict of the individual purpose with a context of human purposes more universal than it. The conflict of Antigone's law of the family with that of the state is the sort of thing he means (though one can question what this implies for the interpretation of the conclusion of that specific play). *Philosophical* awareness that the destruction of individuality is the essence of tragedy becomes possible because 'In its seriousness art for us is something past. For us other forms are necessary to make the divine into our object. We need the thought' (ibid. p. 311–2). Art is still too tied to the world of particular representations, which must themselves be negated if they are to result in a universal concept. Although art is an 'essential manner of representing the divine, and we must understand this form', the real situation is therefore that 'philosophy has to contemplate the truth/what is true (*das Wahrhafte*) in art' (ibid. p. 312) by articulating it in concepts. The link to the 'theoreticist' problem with which we began should be clear.

The historical story of a move from tragedy to philosophy, from myth-based to concept-based explanation, obviously fits the pattern of Hegel's thought, involving a move from what is more 'immediate', particular images and stories, to what is more 'mediated', theories which articulate the universal truth that is inherent in, but not conceptually articulated by, the stories. What, though, of the persistence of tragedy which lies behind Nietzsche's returning of tragedy to the centre of philosophical attention later in the nineteenth century? One of the concerns of the period of philosophy from German Idealism and Romanticism, to Nietzsche and Walter Benjamin is precisely with how modern tragedy relates both to Greek tragedy and to philosophy. Shakespeare plays a pre-eminent role in this issue, frequently being regarded as a kind of test-case for understanding aspects of what differentiates the modern world from the ancient world.

In a piece written in 1771 Goethe suggests the beginning of a framework for the issues here when he maintains that Shakespeare's 'plays all turn around the secret point (which no philosopher has yet seen and determined) in which the particularity of our I, the presumed freedom of our will, clashes with the necessary course of the whole' (Goethe-Berliner Ausgabe Vol. 17 p. 188). The importance of this remark lies in the fact that the philosophical question of free-will and determinism can be seen as being explored by Shakespeare in a way which reveals the impossibility of establishing a fixed division between the internal and the external in accounting for human action. Any attempt to arrive at a philosophical theory with regard to the issue of free-will is therefore likely to conflict with what might be learned from the plays. The historical reception of the plays and the still ongoing debates over the motivation of Hamlet, for example, suggest what this might imply. Even if – per impossibile – a metaphysical account of the issue of freedom came to be universally accepted (and even being clear about what freedom is already suggests the problem), would this give us a way either of deciding on the right interpretation of the play or of dismissing the play for its mistaken account of human action? The absurdity of both alternatives does not, note, stop philosophers in other areas advocating positions which would essentially come down to such alternatives. It is this kind of scepticism with regard to the capacity of modern philosophy to resolve things by knowledge of answers to the contradictions they involve which connects Cavell with figures like Goethe, and the early German Romantics.

In his essay 'Shakespeare und kein Ende!' of 1813 Goethe develops the idea implied by the 'secret point' in relation to the contrast between Shakespeare and Greek tragedy. He here considers the relationship between '*Sollen*', 'ought', and '*Wollen*', 'will', as a means of understanding how ancient tragedy relates to modern tragedy. He uses the metaphor of differing relationships between chance and individual initiative in card-games to elucidate the issue. Some games, like whist, which correspond to the ancient view of things, depend very much on the hand one is dealt. The form of these games 'limits coincidence, indeed limits willing itself. I have, with the people I am playing with and against, to manipulate a long sequence of coincidences with the cards I am dealt, without being able to avoid the coincidences' (Goethe-BA Bd. 18 p. 153). One does what one ought to do in terms of a set of fixed rules governing chance hands of cards that allow for little free decision. Other games – think of poker – where one can, for example, pretend to have a good hand when one has a bad one, and vice versa, and so win by skilful deception, depend on my initiative and so correspond to the modern 'way of thinking and writing' (ibid.). In ancient tragedy the 'despotic' nature we moderns see in the ought is really an expression of the aim of the 'well-being of the whole', as opposed to that of the individual will. This changes the very ways in which action is understood because individual will is not regarded as the essential basis for interpreting action. The argument is like the one we have already seen in Hegel. The problem of tragedy in modernity lies, then, in the domination of individual will: 'Tragedy becomes big and strong by the ought, small and weak by the will' (ibid. p. 154). The significance of Shakespeare lies, Goethe contends, in his attempt to balance ought and will, but will, he maintains, is always at a disadvantage. Goethe's key point – he gives the examples of Hamlet and the ghost, the witches and Lady Macbeth, and of Brutus's friends – is that 'a willing that goes beyond the powers of an individual is modern. But because Shakespeare does not make it arise from within, but excites it by an external cause, this means that it becomes a kind of ought and comes close to antiquity' (ibid. p.155). Like many writers Goethe here seeks to understand how it is that Shakespeare manages to sustain tragedy in a historical situation – that of the emergence of the modern individual – which militates against what was essential to Greek tragedy. The precariousness of the explanation is what makes Shakespeare so intriguing.

The model in which 'inside' and 'outside' involve a changing relationship between the ancient and the modern, and in which Shakespeare is central to an appreciation of the nature of the relationship, recurs in many accounts of Shakespeare and tragedy by philosophers in the German tradition. What is perhaps most interesting here are the differing construals of the significance of the relationship between inside and outside, which often appears as the relationship between freedom and necessity, but which takes one away from the idea of them as two clearly separable, opposed sides. In the 1802–3 *Philosophy of Art*, for example, Schelling says that the tragic person – he is referring to Oedipus – is '*necessarily* guilty of a crime' (Schelling 1/5 p. 695), which appears to characterise the difference between freedom and necessity in a contradictory manner. Schelling sees the hero's freedom as best manifested in their preparedness to take on the consequences of their action even if they intended precisely to avoid the consequences that resulted from it. Richard Eldridge has suggested that 'Tragedy depicts the undoing of *eudaimonia* by the very qualities necessary for its achievement' (Eldridge 2001 p. 151), which suggests how the hero might confront their situation in the manner Schelling suggests is germane to tragedy. Schelling thinks that the tragic hero's accepting the consequences thereby relativises the otherwise 'overwhelming power of fate' (Schelling 1/5 p. 698) and renders their will 'sublime', so manifesting the reconciliation of freedom and necessity that is one of the main aims of German Idealism. Once again it seems clear here that the attempt to understand tragedy may be as important as the philosophical attempt to come to terms with Kant's dualisms in the genesis of this version of how to reconcile the world of freedom and the world of necessity. What, though, of Shakespeare as the representative of modern tragedy?

Schelling claims of Shakespeare that, in line with the modern Protestant conception, 'Character takes the place of the fate of the ancients in him, but he puts such a powerful fate into character that it cannot be attributed to freedom but is present as irresistible necessity' (ibid. p. 720). Whereas Banquo is not affected by the witches, Macbeth is: 'It is therefore character that decides' (ibid. p. 721). The difference of the emphasis on inner and outer from that of Goethe should be clear. The ethical resolution of contradiction which Schelling regards as characteristic of ancient tragedy is broken up in modern tragedy. Where the 'ancient lyre conjured the whole world from four notes; the new instrument has a thousand strings, it splits up the harmony of the universe in order to create it' (ibid. p. 723). The point of what Schelling says about character in Shakespeare is that freedom and necessity in modern tragedy no longer achieve the ancients' higher synthesis of competing necessities, as there are too many competing freedoms. Hegel takes a similar line with regard to modern tragedy: 'the reconciliation is that the individual maintains the formal power of their character; the unity with oneself that is achieved is the formal [i.e. not 'the substantial' that pertains to the community]' (Hegel

2003 p. 308). The result of modern drama is therefore contingent, not necessary, as it is in Greek tragedy: 'This contingency can only become interesting to the extent that it harmonises with what goes on in the mind. Hamlet has no security, the sandbank of finitude is not enough for him. In the background of his mind lies death. And this inner necessity is carried out by contingent externality' (ibid. p. 309). This relationship of inner and outer is crucial.

For Hegel, what he terms 'Romantic art', which conveys the essence of the modern, is characterised by the falling apart of internal and external. The subject no longer relies on an immanent order of things of the kind ancient tragedy both tests most emphatically and yet thereby confirms most emphatically. It is therefore only philosophy that can take on the challenge of the modern situation. Philosophy seeks a new unity, which is to result from going through the divisions inherent in a modernity where pre-established orders can longer lay direct claim to legitimacy and rationality. This unity has to be achieved through the 'exertion of the concept', not manifested in symbolic form as it is in art. However one interprets what Hegel means – is he, for example, in fact referring to the new rigour achieved by the analytical methods of the natural sciences in overcoming mythological and anthropomorphic explanations, or is he just referring to philosophy, and what does this then mean in concrete terms? – the question arises as to whether the state of 'unhappy consciousness', where the subject is inherently at odds with reality, might not in fact be the ineliminable essence of modernity with which we have to come to terms, rather than that which philosophical insight can overcome. The question is then how the 'internal' unhappy consciousness relates to tragedy, which in its ancient form could, in the terms of this conception, have no place even for the very idea of such a consciousness, because it is the product of modern individualism and the falling apart of inside and outside. This brings us to another philosophical perspective on the issues.

It is well known that Hegel both relied a great deal on the Jena Romantics, particularly Friedrich Schlegel, for the development of his ideas, and was then highly critical of what he saw as the consequences of the Romantics' claims, not least because they seemed to exemplify the inherent dissatisfaction associated with the 'unhappy consciousness'. As so often, proximity gives rise to the most emphatic attempts to refute that to which one is so close. The basic difference between them is that Hegel thinks that Schlegel's idea, advanced in lectures which Hegel probably attended, that 'Truth arises when opposed errors neutralise each other' (Schlegel 1991 p. 93) must entail a final position in which the systematic account of 'negation of the negation' enables philosophy to articulate the positive nature of truth. Schlegel, on the other hand, thinks that the idea of opposed errors leads to 'irony', in which determinate claims about the absolute have to be undermined even as they still have to be made. He admits, for example, that 'If all truth is relative, then the proposition is also relative that all truth is relative' (ibid. p. 95), but that does not mean that he thinks the positive, non-relative claim has any substantive content.

One consequence of this way of thinking, which is roughly con-temporaneous with these claims – which ask questions about the very aims of philosophy – appears in Schlegel's account in his *On the Study of Greek Literature* of 1795–7 of the figure of Hamlet:

> The centrepoint of the whole lies in the character of the hero. By a strange situation all the power of his noble nature is compressed into the understanding [i.e. his knowing self], but the capacity for action is completely destroyed. His mind is split, is torn apart, as on the torture rack, in opposing directions; it falls apart and is submerged in the excess of pointless understanding which oppresses him even more than it does those who approach him. There is perhaps no more complete representation of irresolvable disharmony which is the real object of philosophical tragedy than such a boundless disparity between the power of thought and of action as there is in Hamlet's character. The total impression of this tragedy is a *maximum of despair*. All impressions which seem individually to be great and important disappear as trivial in the face of what here appears as the last, sole result of all being and thinking, in the face of the eternal *colossal dissonance* which separates humankind and fate (Schlegel 1971, p. 247–8).

What Schlegel terms 'philosophical tragedy' (in contrast to ancient tragedy) is therefore not constituted in terms of a resolution of contradictions, but is rather based on a 'feeling of *despair*' and involves an 'ethical pain about infinite lack and irresolvable conflict' (ibid. note 5). Aspects of such a view will, as we will see, come to play a role in Walter Benjamin's account of *Trauerspiel*. The desire to achieve the highest in modern art is, Schlegel maintains, faced with the situation that 'The absolutely *highest* can, however, never be completely achieved. The most that the striving force is capable of is: to approximate ever more and more to this unachievable goal. And even this *endless approximation* does not seem to be without inner contradictions' (ibid. p. 255). This is because the idea of a continuous progress, which might be applied to the sciences, does not harmonise with the nature of the truth he thinks art should convey, or with the sense that it is often the contingency of circumstances that leads to great art. It is not that Schlegel harks back here to a golden age when art reflected a harmonious human existence, as is sometimes thought of 'Romanticism'. His concern is with the *future* of modern culture and he speculates on the need for an 'objective' theory of literature and art that would come to terms both with the fact that modern art is inherently reflexive, 'sentimental' rather than 'naïve', and with the demand that art be more than mere subjective projection.

The complexities of Schlegel's response to questions of modern art and tragedy are too great to explore here. I want briefly just to consider a few implications of the paradigmatic tension that is present in aspects of the relationship between Hegel's idealist conception of modern tragedy and Schlegel's suspicion of the philosophical resolution of the irresolvable conflict in modern tragedy. The basic reason for the tension is simple: Schlegel's view of philosophy leads to art, whereas Hegel's view of art leads to philosophy. Schlegel sees the absolute as a regulative idea that is generated by the failure of foundationalism in modern philosophy, and this is what generates his ambivalent responses to a work like *Hamlet*, which takes the negative consequences of such failure to the limit.

81

What prevents him renouncing thinking and descending into Hamlet's despair is the idea that the relativity of all particular truths can only ever be continually experienced in the failure of the attempt to get beyond that relativity. This idea is essential to the experience of art, and is not something which philosophy can express. He talks in this connection of 'the higher scepticism of Socrates, which, unlike common scepticism, does not consist in the denial of truth and certainty, but rather in the serious search for them' (Schlegel 1964 p. 202). Hegel thinks problems of grounding and of scepticism can be obviated by the realisation that the fact, upon which the sceptic relies, that truth is only the result of the refutation of what has previously been held as true precisely leads to the ultimate truth that there can be no legitimation outside the practices of human communities, hence his conception of tragedy.

What both are concerned with can be seen in terms of the issue of nihilism that is raised by F.H. Jacobi in the 1780s and 1790s:

> man loses himself as soon as he refuses to find himself, in a manner which is incomprehensible to his reason, in God as his maker, as soon as he wishes to ground himself *in himself alone*. Everything then dissolves into his own nothingness. But man has the following choice, and only this choice: *nothingness* or a *God*. If he chooses nothingness he makes *himself* into God; that means: he makes God into a *phantasm* (*Gespenst*); for it is impossible, if there is no God, that man and all that surrounds him should not be merely a *phantasm* (Jacobi 1799 p. 48–9).

The resonances with Schlegel's characterisation of Hamlet seem fairly clear, despite Jacobi's theological alternative. Jacobi forms a vital aspect of that side of modern philosophy which realises, as Cavell puts it, that 'the human creature's basis in the world as a whole, its relation to the world as such is, is not that of knowing, anyway not what we think of as knowing' (Cavell 1979 p. 241). As Jacobi contends: 'I understand by the true something which is *before* and *outside* knowledge; which first gives a value to knowledge and to the *capacity* for knowledge, to *reason*' (Jacobi 1799 p. 27).

Jacobi's argument that any attempt at grounding our knowledge leads to a regress recurs in Nietzsche's *Birth of Tragedy*, but Nietzsche thinks that what for Jacobi was the ground of a faith in reason, 'the true', is actually the 'Dionysian', which destroys 'the usual barriers and limits of existence' (Nietzsche 2000 Vol. 1 p. 48). Nietzsche regards the 'Dionysian person' as like Hamlet: 'both have once gained a true insight into the essence of things, they have *realised* ('*erkannt*'), and to act disgusts them; for their action can change nothing of the eternal essence of things, they feel it to be ridiculous or shameful that they are supposed to restore the world which is out of joint' (ibid.). At this point in his career Nietzsche, unlike Schopenhauer and in some respects like Schlegel, thinks that art gives one a reason for living on, an aesthetic 'justification' of existence, even though it is only illusion/appearance. The later Nietzsche characteristically maintains in *Ecce Homo* that 'It is precisely tragedy which is the proof that the Greeks were not pessimists: Schopenhauer got it wrong here, in the way he got everything wrong' (ibid. Vol. 2 p. 1108–9). By this time he opposes Dionysus to 'the Crucified' as the manifestation of 'a curse on life' (i.e. Christianity), maintaining that 'Dionysus who is cut into pieces is a *promise* ('*Verheissung*') of life: it will eternally be born again and come home from destruction' (ibid. Vol. 3, p. 774). The question is, he maintains, whether the meaning of suffering should be regarded in a 'Christian' or a 'tragic' manner, the former seeking for an answer beyond life, the latter seeing meaning in this life, there being no other life, and no need or reason to justify life. Shakespeare does not play a major role in the later Nietzsche. The following remark suggests why. Nietzsche's Greek perspective on things puts anything associated with Christian culture into question: 'just say the word "Dionysos" before the best recent names and things, before Goethe, or Beethoven, or Shakespeare, or Raphael: and suddenly we feel our best things and moments *judged* [in the sense that they do not live up to what Dionysus signified for Greek culture]' (ibid. Vol. 3 p. 463).

It is a banality to suggest that Christian culture is in some respects a counter to Greek tragic culture, but this banality would help to explain Nietzsche's largely unargued objections to so much modern culture. The issue of Shakespearean tragedy and modern philosophy is significant, though, because it demands a much more differentiated approach than is to be found in Nietzsche. As we have seen, much turns upon different construals of the relationship between individual and community, inside and outside, freedom and necessity, which are, precisely, some of the most intractable issues in modernity.

To this extent one can hardly hope to arrive at any worthwhile general conclusions, so I want instead to point briefly to one issue from a particular perspective which seems to me to offer some possible future perspectives on the relationship between Shakespeare, modern and ancient tragedy, and philosophy. The issue arises from a connection between some remarks by Cavell on music and Shakespeare, and Walter Benjamin's insistence in the 1920s on a radical distinction between tragedy and *Trauerspiel* (a word whose meaning is probably best captured by Gillian Rose's 'play of mourning'). In case this topic seems rather abstruse in the present context, what is at issue is the relationship of the rise of the 'autonomous' music which reaches its peak from Beethoven to Mahler, to the decline of tragedy in modernity, in which Shakespeare plays a pivotal role. The importance of music in this respect is that the historical change in its status that occurs roughly in the period of Romanticism, which can, though, perhaps be seen to be prepared somewhat earlier, offers a way of considering Cavell's remarks about the 'moral' or 'truth of scepticism', cited above. Cavell claims, as we saw, that 'the human creature's basis in the world as a whole, its relation to the world as such is, is not that of knowing, anyway not what we think of as knowing' (Cavell 1979 p. 241), and that when, with Descartes, philosophy becomes obsessively concerned with using knowledge to ground that basis, the problem of our place in things becomes acute. The obvious point about music is that it is not in any epistemological sense a form of knowing, and involves a kind of connection to the world which cannot be reduced to what we know about it, namely the connection of 'feeling'. The issue of feeling and tragedy leads us to Benjamin.

Benjamin's writings on tragedy and Trauerspiel are in general more admired than they are understood, and I can only scratch the surface of a very small part of them here.[7] The basis of Benjamin's investigations is the claim that 'the modern stage does not present any tragedy which resembles that of the Greeks' (Benjamin 1980 I.I p. 280). In its most strict version his argument means that there simply is no modern tragedy, because there is no grounded modern world order. In this respect some of Cavell's argument is therefore the opposite of Benjamin's – though this may in one respect be just a dispute about words – as for him tragedy is the 'interpretation of what skepticism is itself an interpretation of' (Cavell 2003 p. 5), which is an essentially modern problem. For Benjamin, whereas Greek tragedy is constituted in language in which 'the word as pure carrier of its meaning is the pure word' (Benjamin 1980 II.1 p. 138), 'the linguistic principle of Trauerspiel', the modern form, is 'the word in transformation' (ibid.): meaning becomes temporalised and unstable. Tragedy is founded on the 'lawfulness' (Gesetzlichkeit) of dialogue. Dialogue in this specific sense does not depend upon the intentions and feelings of the individuals engaged in that dialogue, because they are located in a context which transcends them, the context of fate, which leads, Benjamin will suggest in the Trauerspielbuch, to the ultimate silence of the hero in tragedy.[8] Trauerspiel, on the other hand, is able to balance 'the capacity of language and of hearing' and so can be expressive: 'indeed in the end everything depends upon the ear of lament, for only lament which has been taken up and heard in the deepest way becomes music. Where in tragedy the eternal rigidity of the spoken word asserts itself (sich erhebt), Trauerspiel gathers the endless resonance of its sound (Klang)' (ibid. II.I p. 140). Meaning that had been grounded in

---

[7] I have looked at them in some detail in Bowie 1997.

[8] Benjamin does not accept that there is any reconciliation involved in the hero's fate in relation to a higher state of the community as had Hegel argued.

a fixed world-order gives way to a divorce of sound and meaning which is manifested in the growing importance of music in the early modern period and beyond.

The less esoteric version of the complex story Benjamin tells would be that there is a shift in the understanding of the nature of language in modernity that results from the idea of the loss of grounded meaning. The disseminatory proliferation of significations characteristic of allegory – think of Shakespeare's use of metaphor, or of metaphysical poetry – is an indication of an ontological change in language, in which 'Every person, every thing, every relationship can arbitrarily mean something else. This possibility passes a devastating but just judgement on the profane world: it is characterised as a world in which details are not strictly that important' (ibid. I.1 p. 350). The last part of this remark seems, though, very questionable, and relies on Benjamin's adherence to a cabbalistic idea of the true divine language whose signification is, unlike language in the modernity represented by allegory, not subject to the arbitrariness of the signifier. His remark that 'As humankind steps out of the pure language of the name it makes language into a means (namely of a cognition which is inappropriate to it), thereby in one part at least into a mere sign ... the origin of abstraction as a capacity of the spirit of language may also be sought in the Fall' (ibid. p. 152–4) suggests his position reasonably clearly. If one takes Cavell's line, though, the modern situation makes details absolutely crucial, if endlessly problematic, even though Cavell is addressing much the same issue. Language as a 'mere sign' is part of the sceptical problematic, as Benjamin's idea of language as the means of cognition suggests.

Benjamin and Cavell, then, concur on differing versions of a related idea, namely that respectively Trauerspiel, and Shakespearean tragedy – Benjamin seems to include the latter in Trauerspiel at times – relate to the problem of grounding in modern philosophy and the consequences of this for leading a human life. (I have shown elsewhere, in Bowie 1997, just how much Benjamin relies on the Romantic version of this

issue which derives from Jacobi's revival of sceptical regress arguments.)
Benjamin connects this theme to the change in the status of music which
leads away from his mythological idea of 'pure language'. The separation
of sound and meaning, which is part of the separation of the word from
a metaphysical order of meaning, makes 'music the opponent of speech,
which is loaded with meaning' (GS I 1. p. 385). At the end of the 17th
century this leads, Benjamin maintains, to the 'dissolution of Trauerspiel
into opera' (ibid.). Despite his critical assessment of opera itself, as a
'product of the decay' of Trauerspiel, he regards music as inextricably related to Trauerspiel: music is 'inwardly familiar in its essence with allegorical drama' (ibid. p. 387). This is because it partakes of the death of
metaphysically grounded meaning which is the core of his interpretation
of Trauerspiel in contrast to tragedy. How this relates to Benjamin's wider
thoughts would take us beyond the scope of what can be attempted here.
The contrast with Cavell can, though, shed some light on Shakespeare
and philosophy.

Cavell's version of this issue appears when he considers the idea that
Shakespeare's kind of drama can be connected to music and links this idea
to the notion that such drama comes to an end precisely at the time – in
which Shakespeare, Bacon, Galileo and Descartes are contemporaries –
of the rise of the epistemological problematic which leads to a 'loss of
presentness' (Cavell 2003 p. 94). The music Cavell refers to is that of
Beethoven, which he thinks shares with Shakespeare's drama a *directed
motion*: 'We do not know where this motion can stop and we do not
understand why it has begun here, so we do not know where we stand or
why we are there' (ibid. p. 92). The basic point, as I understand it, is that
the drama and the music demand a form of attention which gives rise
to immanent meaning – 'presentness' – which is possible only inasmuch
as it is not knowledge. In Cavell's version of the issues we have observed
in Benjamin, drama after Shakespeare 'lost the use of poetry and turned
to music' (ibid. p. 123). The loss of presentness will later occur in music
with the move to atonality. The important music that Cavell intends

therefore takes over from verbal language as the medium of dramatising a human existence which can no longer be adequately articulated in verbal form. I have no simple answer to what this signifies for the self-understanding of modern philosophy, but the constellation seems vital to me if we are not to remain trapped in an epistemologically exclusive paradigm of philosophy. The questions for philosophy which emerge from this constellation are central to the future of the humanities at a time when the failure to legitimate one's activity in terms of knowledge is increasingly seen as a failure to contribute to the prevailing social goals. The relationships between tragedy, philosophy and music provoked by the attempt to respond adequately to Shakespeare serve as a reminder of how distorted perceptions of social progress may have become.

References

Benjamin, Walter (1980) *Gesammelte Schriften*, (Frankfurt: Suhrkamp)

Bowie, Andrew (1997) *From Romanticism to Critical Theory. The Philosophy of German Literary Theory*, (London: Routledge)

Cavell, Stanley (1976) *Must we mean what we say?*, (Cambridge: Cambridge University Press)

Cavell, Stanley (2003) *Disowning Knowledge: In Seven Plays of Shakespeare*, (Cambridge: Cambridge University Press)

Eldridge, Richard (2001) *The Persistence of Romanticism*, (Cambridge: Cambridge University Press)

Goethe, J.W. v quotations from Goethe, *Berliner Ausgabe*, in *Deutsche Literatur von Lessing bis Kafka*, (Berlin: Directmedia)

Hegel, G.W.F (1970) *Phänomenologie des Geistes*, (Frankfurt: Suhrkamp)

Hegel, G.W.F. (2003) *Vorlesungen über die Philosophie der Kunst*, (Hamburg: Meiner)

Jacobi, Friedrich Heinrich (1799) *Jacobi an Fichte*, (Hamburg: Friedrich Perthes)

Nietzsche, Friedrich (2000) *Werke*, (ed. Schlechta), (Berlin: Directmedia)

Schelling, F.W.J. (1856–61) *Friedrich Wilhelm Joseph Schelling's Sämmtliche Werke*, ed. K.F.A. Schelling, I Abtheilung Vols. 1–10, II Abtheilung Bde. 1–4, (Stuttgart: Cotta)

Schelling, F.W.J. (1969) *Initia Philosophiae Universae* (1820–1), ed. Horst Fuhrmans, (Bonn: Bouvier)

Schlegel, Friedrich (1964) *Philosophische Vorlesungen* (1800–1807) (*Kritische Friedrich Schlegel Ausgabe* Vol. 12), (Munich, Paderborn, Vienna: Ferdinand Schöningh)

Schlegel, Friedrich (1971) *Kritische Friedrich Schlegel Ausgabe* Volume 1, (Munich, Paderborn, Vienna: Ferdinand Schöningh

Schlegel, Friedrich (1991) *Transcendentalphilosophie*, ed. Michael Elsässer, (Hamburg: Meiner)

HISTORY AND METAPHILOSOPHY

The perceptive title of the conference at which the first version of this piece was given, 'The Philosophy of the History of Philosophy', sums up the problem which is the concern of this essay. One way of suggesting the problem is simple: the 'Philosophy' which reflects on the 'history of philosophy' seems to have to be of a different order from that of which it is the philosophy. It arguably has to be an absolute that contrasts with something relative, in the form of the philosophies which have a history, including those which previously saw themselves as taking the role of being philosophies of the history of philosophy. (These only began to exist, of course, at the earliest in the second half of the 18th century.) The really blunt version of this problem is, then, that the Philosophy of the history of philosophy has to be true, in contrast to the philosophies of which it is the Philosophy, which are now in some way false. This is one way in which Hegel's philosophy has been interpreted, though we shall see a very different way in a moment. If one does not wish to make this absolute claim – and these days many people tend to feel uncomfortable about doing so – the blunt alternative is to admit that one's own position as part of the history of philosophy is just one of the relative positions which make up this history. Doing this has the unsatisfactory consequence of making it hard to explain why what one is doing is philosophy, on the assumption that if philosophy is not about truth it is hard to say what makes it philosophy at all. This is all, of course, rather schematic and imprecise, because the terms I am using have not been properly examined, but the something like this dilemma has played a significant role in the history of modern philosophy.

One familiar response to this dilemma is to say that the history of philosophy is really the 'history of ideas', whereas philosophy deals with the best answers to the real philosophical problems of the present. The cruder versions of this strategy, the strategy in those kinds of analytical philosophy which think of themselves as doing what natural scientists do when they produce a theory of something, are increasingly discredited. This is not least because there is such a diversity of opposed conceptions of any significant philosophical issue (let alone of interpretations of those conceptions) that the claim to be in possession of the best answer, of the kind a physicist might make about quantum mechanics, can rightly be greeted with suspicion. We don't really know what philosophical confirmation is, apart from in relation to some contentless issues in formal logic, whereas we do know that good scientific theories are confirmed by their predictive and explanatory power. This is not to say that there may not be such a best philosophical answer – to claim that would just repeat the same problem the other way round – but it is to say that the division between the history of ideas and 'real' philosophy is based on a claim which is not legitimated by the making of the division. How do we tell when real philosophy is being done, rather than mere history of ideas, if not on the circular premise that, for example, 'real philosophers' are doing it? This is, it is worth remembering, how it works in the academic world: for years people have failed to get jobs because they were supposedly doing the history of ideas and not real philosophy.

However, the signal failure of the more ambitious aims of the in-augurators of the analytical tradition to achieve what they set out to achieve, by showing, in Moritz Schlick's words, that 'the fate of all "philosophical problems" is this: Some of them will disappear by being shown to be mistakes and misunderstandings of our language and the others will be shown to be ordinary scientific questions in disguise' (in ed. Rorty 1992 p. 51) should be a warning against the glib adoption of the division between philosophy and the history of ideas. Many of the problems Schlick thought could be solved are precisely those which led to the demise of his project: language turned out not to have the relationship to the data of science he thought it did. Crucially for my argument the reasons why this is so were already mapped out, for example, by Schleiermacher in the first half of the 19th century – he uses the same argument as Quine does against the analytic-synthetic distinction – but his arguments were ignored by the analytical tradition until Quine unconsciously repeated them.

Another response to the dilemma is to claim that Philosophy, which in this context is often called 'metaphysics' – particularly by those in the traditions following Heidegger – is therefore something which people have pursued in the hope of arriving somewhere which is not merely a contingent part of history generated by the human desire to dominate the other, the desire to make the different into the same. The realisation that this is what Philosophy is brings Philosophy to an end, in the name of what Heidegger terms 'thinking'. The crude objection to this position is that it is making an absolute claim to the effect that everything is relative, so that it involves a performative contradiction, or falls prey to the standard objection to relativism. However, the fact that rejections of metaphysics end up in paradox if they try to make universal claims, does not exclude the possibility that strategies might be found to circumvent the problems of *asserting* that metaphysics, in the sense presupposed by the idea of the Philosophy of the history of philosophy, has come to an end. This would involve a negative realisation that an overarching view of truth we may come to be convinced by is just the result of the revelation that the alternatives offered during the history of philosophy are unsustainable. The status of this realisation is the problem, but some of the attempts to work out such a position are characteristic of the recent re-interpretations of Hegel in the light of contemporary pragmatism. The very fact that Hegel can figure both as the ultimate positive metaphysician, and as a serious candidate for being the first to suggest how the 'end of philosophy' might look, is a crucial part of what I want to investigate.

The preceding remarks involve aspects of three rough alternatives, between (1) a version of Hegelianism, which seeks to overcome the problem of philosophy's history via an absolutised metaphilosophy that provides the 'context of all contexts' (Habermas), i.e. the most obvious case of the Philosophy of the history of philosophy; (2) an analytical approach which thinks it can isolate real philosophical problems from the contingency of history; and (3) a version of Nietzsche's attack on metaphysics which can be see as either entailing a metaphilosophical claim to a position beyond or after philosophy, or as circumventing the whole problem by refusing to engage with standard forms of philosophical argumentation in the name of a transformation of human practices. As just presented, none of these is necessarily a wholly attractive proposition, and ultimately I do not think that they are. There are, however, as we shall see, versions of such positions which still offer a great deal of illumination of what is at issue here.

A key thought which illuminates the philosophical status of trying to do the history of philosophy can be approached via a remark of Friedrich Schlegel's in the *Athenaeum*: 'Demonstrations in philosophy are just demonstrations in the sense of the language of the art of military strategy (*im Sinne der militärischen Kunstsprache*). It is no better with [philosophical] deductions than with political ones; in the sciences as well one first of all occupies a terrain and then proves one's right to it afterwards' (Schlegel 1988 Vol. 2 p. 111. 'Deduction' is being used in the legal sense adopted by Kant, meaning 'legitimation'). Schlegel's remark – which may well be referring to Fichte's 'self-positing' I that tries to establish itself as the ground of philosophy – suggests an alternative to the positions just observed (though it comes close to number (3)). Take the following example. If one looks at the origins of analytical philosophy the arguments used against Hegelianism in logical empiricism all in fact fall prey to one of Hegel's own most plausible arguments, namely the argument against the 'myth of the given' in the 'Sense Certainty' section of the *Phenomenology*. This is why the work of Wilfrid Sellars has become so important in contemporary philosophy. Hegel's argument simply says that apparent immediate non-inferential certainty in sensuous perception does not provide a criterion of knowledge. Sense data can only be truth-determinate because they inherently involve conceptual content, and this means they do not provide the pure 'given' which, along with the laws of logic, analytical philosophy initially thought was the only basis of philosophical certainty. There is no doubt at all that the analytical philosophy which began in this unpromising manner, by writing off the philosophy which was to prove right against it, did 'occupy the terrain' and only afterwards tried to prove its right to the terrain – to the point, of course, where what began in this way dominated much of world philosophy. However, my somewhat tendentious presentation of the origins of analytical philosophy fails to give any sense of what made its success possible. What sort of grounds can one validly adduce for an explanation here, and how do they relate to the Philosophy of the history of philosophy? It is worth adding that Schlegel's claim may be the only way one can really do philosophy, i.e. by beginning with some kind of 'intuition', which one then tries to legitimate. Indeed, a great deal of analytical philosophy in recent years has been predicated on the idea that one's job is to 'pump up' intuitions (which has, perhaps understandably, led to a counter-reaction, which seeks to return us to the certainties promised by metaphysics).

The most plausible response to the question of what enabled the analytical approach to succeed is simply to cite the close link between the natural sciences and the philosophers of logical empiricism. Even though their philosophical arguments turn out to be implausible, their attachment to plausible science gave them credibility. In that case, though, the answer is merely ideological, and offers little for the question of the Philosophy of the history of philosophy, beyond an essentially Nietzschean story about power and discourse. One might therefore also construe the answer in terms of a 'hermeneutic of suspicion' of a Marxist kind, which is in fact what the Frankfurt School did in relation to the Vienna Circle, despite the fact that their initial political aims were not very far apart from each other. This construal of the analytical tradition would, no doubt, scandalise many philosophers, though it is worth noting that Hilary Putnam claims of the contemporary end of analytical philosophy in the old style that 'Analytic philosophy has already begun to lose shape as a tendency with the disappearance of a strong ideological current at its center' (Putnam 1983 p. 303). Those attached to that tradition will refer to the advances in logic by Frege and others, and to the new rigour of argument involved in analytical philosophy. It is arguable, though, that these advances also have a down-side because they exclude so many other approaches to the philosophical understanding of language and other issues, and because they can (but need not) contribute to the rise of the scientism which Putnam sees as such a threat to contemporary culture. The decision on such matters is, of course, metaphilosophical, and this just returns us to the basic problem that the metaphilosophical position might be just as contingent as what it opposes.

Is it the case, then, that there can be no such thing as philosophical progress, because, as Schlegel's remark suggests, the metaphilosophical assumptions by which such progress might be gauged keep shifting with history? Is the difficulty of establishing metaphilosophical perspectives actually itself the indication of the end of philosophy, in the name of some 'post-modern' alternative? What is at issue here seems to me to be located between versions of quite loosely construed, Kantian, Hegelian, and Nietzschean thought. One way to show this is to look at some issues raised by the most plausible version of contemporary Hegelianism, which is one form of opposition to the Nietzschean perspective. The point of this interpretation of Hegel is that it accepts the critique of metaphysical foundationalism and seeks its philosophical resources in the real historical world. The underlying issue is how to deal with the contingency this involves, a contingency which, as this interpretation argues, may actually have certain limits. The fact that there are such limits offers hope for a defensible metaphilosophical stance.

Terry Pinkard epitomises the deflationary interpretation of Hegel in the following description of what he thinks absolute spirit means: 'the human community comes to an awareness that it is in working out the internal requirements of its own reason-giving activity that it sets for itself what is to count for it as its absolute principles' (Pinkard 1996 p. 254). The Philosophy of the history of philosophy is therefore the result of an *immanent* negotiation within the human community. The key element of Hegel stressed in this interpretation is his insistence on immanence. Pinkard, then, as does Robert Pippin, regards Hegel as the most important thinker of a self-legislating modernity. The absolute position that overcomes the relativity of history is actually the result of there no longer being any possibility of appealing to a transcendent authority. Communities must have recourse to intersubjective agreement without invoking anything outside what they can work out within their own institutions. Hegel's idea of thought's 'self-determination' need not, then, be read as though there were an immanent driving force of rationality, called *Geist*, which forces us to acknowledge that the 'real is the rational'. The idea instead designates the recognition on our part that, as Pippin puts it, 'we always require ... a narrative account of why we have come to regard some set of rules or a practice as authoritative' (Pippin 1999 p. 68). There can be no other form of legitimation, because that would involve an appeal to something transcendent.

In this view the Philosophy of the history of philosophy is itself the legitimation of human practices, presumably including philosophy itself. The idea of all-inclusive immanence therefore no longer forces one to invoke obscure notions like the 'self-determination of the concept', because what is at stake amounts to the fact that legitimation of all kinds in modernity has to include reflection on the sources of our decisive notions in the concrete history of a human community. What makes the argument really interesting is the following claim. The task of philosophy is seen as showing that there is a wider development of rationality in modernity, evident, for example, in things which have become impossible to justify, like slavery and the oppression of women. The very impossibility of now finding an intersubjective justification for such things is the final court of appeal. However, this court does not have transcendent authority, and its justifications can always be revised in terms of a better, more inclusive, narrative of legitimation. There are clearly problems with this, because the decision on the narrative of legitimation will always be contested from some quarter. At the same time, the intuition behind this position is very powerful, both in relation to cognitive and ethical issues: there are, quite simply, things which it is inconceivable could ever be legitimated again. Obviously this is not an empirical claim: supporters of fundamentalist Islam will no doubt contest the issue of women, but the claim is that if they were prepared to enter an all-inclusive discussion they could not substantiate their case. Despite this important claim there are two productive objections that can be made to this position. One comes from Habermas' broadly 'Kantian', and the other from Rorty's broadly 'Nietzschean' position.

Habermas has objected to this account of Hegel by pointing out that

> Even from the point of view of a completely inclusive community there is an *unmediated* difference between the social world which we share intersubjectively and the objective world with which we are confronted and have to cope. Just as little can, secondly, the tension between what is valid 'for us' and what is valid 'in and for itself' be removed. What is rationally acceptable according to our lights is not necessarily the same as what is objectively true (Habermas 1999 p. 218–9).

We cannot anticipate what the completion of knowledge could look like, because our knowledge is arrived at by explaining what we encounter contingently in nature in the form of fallible consensuses about what there is. The recent attempts to convert Hegel's conception of 'absolute knowledge' into an account of intersubjective agreement are consequently, Habermas claims, both inaccurate as an account of what Hegel could have meant and inadequate to the nature of 'post-metaphysical' rationality. The attempts are inaccurate because Hegel does lay claim to a completed *philosophical* knowledge at the end of the system, to a 'context of all contexts' (ibid.).

The Hegelian Philosophy of the history of philosophy is arrived at by explicating all the ways in which thought and its object can be in contradiction, and by then revealing how the contradictions are necessarily overcome. What is actually, in Hegel's own terms, objective spirit, in the sense of the contingent, socially-located historical manifestations of our conceptions, is, Habermas argues, taken by Hegel as absolute spirit. Hegel, then, ignores the genesis of spirit in specific historical contexts and therefore regards it as thought's own complete self-understanding. This stance is therefore inadequate to the 'post-metaphysical' situation because it conflates fallible rational acceptability in an all-inclusive community with the – Kantian – regulative idea of absolute validity. For Habermas this regulative idea arises from the 'cooperative search for truth' (ibid. p. 221) of historically contingent individuals who seek to transcend their contingency by extending the contexts of their knowledge, even though they can never *know* if anything is absolutely valid: 'nothing gives us the right to expect that we will have the last word' (ibid. p. 209). In short, the notion of consensus alone fails to take account of the absolute conception of truth which transcends all particular contexts. (This is one of Habermas' corrections to his own earlier view of the 'ideal speech situation'.) Habermas regards the absolute conception of truth as an essentially *normative*, not a substantive notion, and argues that Hegel lays claim to it in an invalid manner by blurring the line between absolute and objective spirit, in order to incorporate the transcendence of truth into his immanent conception.

The lurking problem in Habermas' alternative is susceptible to both a Hegelian and a Nietzschean interpretation, and it is arguable that Rorty tries to combine the two. The simplest way to see the problem lies in Rorty's objections to Habermas' assumption of the transcendence of truth, which makes it into a regulative idea. Rorty claims that 'all I can mean by "transcendent" is "getting beyond our present practices by a gesture in the direction of our possibly different future practices"' (Rorty 1998 p.61), so that the fallibilist 'cautionary' use of 'true' is just a 'gesture towards future generations' (ibid. p. 60), rather than something which relies on the assumption that there is an ultimate 'objective' 'fact of the matter'. There may in future be what, for the future, is a better way of going about some discursive or other practice, but what makes it better is not a transcendent fact. For Habermas, in contrast, 'It is the goal of justifications to find out a truth which stretches beyond all justifications' (Habermas 1999 p. 53), i.e. the goal is something transcendent.

This latter stance suggests that there must be some other way of arriving at truth beyond justification, but the problem is that Habermas does not specify what it is. Rorty, on the other hand, thinks that even though 'any discursive practice will necessarily have an "is-seems" distinction' (Rorty 1998 p. 167), *the **only** point in contrasting the true with the merely justified is to contrast a possible future with the actual present* (Rorty 1999 p. 39). The regulative idea of truth for Rorty is 'an ever-retreating goal, one that fades forever and forever when we move'. This is, he argues, 'not what common sense would call a goal. For it is neither something we might realise we had reached, nor something to which we might get closer' (Rorty 1998 p. 39). Rorty does, though, claim that the notion of a goal of inquiry or a moral ideal which is supposed to be endlessly approached but never attained is a useful *focus imaginarius*, albeit one which 'is none the worse for being an invention rather than (as Kant thought it) a built in feature of the human mind' (Rorty 1989 p. 196). However, at the same time, Rorty himself admits that '"true" is an absolute term' (Rorty 1998 p. 2), claiming that 'Davidson has helped us realize that *the very absoluteness of truth is a good reason for thinking "true" indefinable and for thinking that no theory of the nature of truth is possible*. It is only the relative about which there is anything to say' (ibid. p. 3). How does this all fit together? The way the contrast between absolute and relative is construed is the key issue.

Let us see, then, how Rorty's claims a) translate into Hegelian and Nietzschean terms, and b) how they translate into the question of the Philosophy of the history of philosophy. Rorty's position is thoroughly immanent, in the manner of Pinkard's and Pippin's Hegelianism. It involves the assumption of a narrative of legitimation that offers a fallible justification of our current assumptions and practices. At the same time Rorty also assumes truth is an absolute notion. Rorty is trying to meet what is inherent in Habermas' objection that Hegelianism conflates objective and absolute spirit by absolutising contingent local consensus. The claim that such consensus is the only absolute does entail the relativist problem: is the claim itself the result of the community of Hegelians claiming to be absolutely inclusive? Consensuses can always turn out to be false. In Habermas' case, the truth is therefore a regulative idea which is a normative limit on what we can legitimately claim, and it is therefore inaccessible but ineluctable. We have already seen Rorty's objection to regulative ideas, which is essentially Nietzsche's objection to the true world that has become a fable. Rorty does, though, avoid the more questionable sides of Nietzsche, where, for example, truth can become just a function of the will to power, and so plays the role of the absolute in an indefensible manner.

Rorty's absolute is inaccessible to philosophy, not in any mystical sense, but simply because of the Davidsonian sense that truth and meaning are inseparable. If we didn't understand what it is for something to be true we would in these terms never understand anything, and the theory of truth therefore has to presuppose the condition of its own possibility. This means it cannot be a theory in the sense that any theory of something in the world can: the latter depend on norms for talking about their object, whereas there cannot be a norm for truth that doesn't just presuppose it. The simple underlying point is that saying 'snow is white' is 'true' just does not mean 'I think snow is white, but I may be wrong about this at some point in the future'. The reason for Rorty's way of putting the issue has to do with his 'Nietzschean' rejection of the correspondence theory of truth (which Habermas, somewhat ambiguously, also rejects). The basis of the rejection is that what we say is part of what constitutes what is true, there being no way of separating the 'scheme' of language from the 'content' of the world. This, though, starts to sound like Hegel again, and the question is how one circumvents the questionable implications of Hegel's metaphilosophy.

What does this all tell us about the Philosophy of the history of philosophy? Let's return to a rather crude threefold model. A 'Kantian' view sees this Philosophy as a regulative idea, and this contrasts with the immanentist Hegelian conception. In the 'Kantian' view whatever philosophical account of the history of philosophy we arrive at is contingent on the state of research, the developments in philosophy, etc., and is fallibilist, open to revision, but with the constant reminder that it is not *the* Philosophy. The 'Hegelian' view thinks this means that the regulative idea is a kind of abstract 'Sollen' which plays no real role in what philosophers actually do, which is to seek an inclusive consensus based on our best practices, there being nothing outside this process. The extreme 'Nietzschean' view sees the history of philosophy as an arbitrary battle-ground where even the progressive rationality claimed by the Hegelian position, in which some things become ethically or cognitively impossible to legitimate, seems to have no purchase, because all that is really at issue are quanta of the will to power. The more moderate Nietzschean view might suggest that the enterprise of the Philosophy of the history of philosophy seeks to make an absolute goal out of something inherently relative: by forgetting that the very idea of such a Philosophy is dependent upon what has contingently developed as philosophy, it seeks a metaphilosophical perspective where the hoped-for truth about itself will emerge.

However, such a typology is in key respects too abstract, and responding to this problem takes the issue to a different level. Reflection on how to think about the history of philosophy must also take account of how goals are pursued in the actual practice of philosophy. The history of the philosophy of science is, for example, littered with failed accounts of such topics as the 'logic of scientific discovery' which can easily be shown to bear little or no relation to what actually happens in real scientific discovery. If one does not assume that the present state of a certain version of key philosophical issues is the norm by which the past is judged – an assumption that the least awareness of the history of philosophy itself should be enough to challenge – the task of the history of philosophy must be seen in terms of inherently conflicting norms. The difficulty here is pretty fundamental because one is faced with essential decisions on what philosophy is supposed to be doing, and trying to overcome the inherent contradictions involved by simply adopting one or other side of the contradiction seems to me the wrong approach. Clearly, working with the assumption that one is doomed to failure, because the contradictions may not be resolvable, is not going to maximise a certain kind of intellectual motivation, but there is a naïveté in assuming that one is excepted from the way in which subsequent philosophy will necessarily invalidate many of the assumptions of one's era. In methodological terms the very awareness, which can be seen in 'Kantian', 'Hegelian', or 'Nietzschean' terms, of how the terms of the debate can move is part of serious investigation of the history of philosophy. The contemporary revival of German Idealism as a response to the failures of empiricist assumptions discussed above is motivated both by objections to the 'myth of the given', the perceived failure of causal explanations of perception and cognition at the level of philosophical argument, and by a sense of wider cultural problems. The latter do manifest themselves in the detail of the arguments, but they also require a perspective that links the arguments to the broader exploration of the reasons for the growing contemporary dominance of reductionist naturalist explanations with respect to the human world, where such explanations very often do not belong. This wider perspective is never going to be easy to achieve without running the risk of reductive generalisation, but one thing it should draw on are precisely earlier manifestations of related philosophical tendencies made available by appropriate attention to the history of philosophy.

This seems to me to have a consequence that undermines any attempt to make an essential separation between philosophy and the history of ideas, of the kind, for example, which assumes that conceptual truths form the object of philosophy. The key concepts involved in such debates are evidently ones which emerge in specific contexts which affect their very content: whilst it is possible to argue using the presently constituted meanings of such concepts, the implications of the argument are at some stage likely to involve reflection on how the concepts came to be used in the way they are now, otherwise their implications will not be fully understood. Why, for example, did the now deeply problematic concept of 'sense datum' emerge at a particular time and come to dominate many assumptions about epistemology, before the questioning of the notion present in Kant and German Idealism was revived? Why, when Schleiermacher questioned it in his *Dialectic*, did it take Quine's almost identical questioning of the analytic/synthetic distinction for the distinction's foundational role to be put in doubt? The answer to such questions involves addressing both the philosophical arguments and their embeddedness in social, scientific, political, and cultural contexts. An unresolved tension is present here between the desire to advance cogent philosophical arguments that cannot constantly look over their shoulders at their genesis or their predecessors and their extra-philosophical implications, and the need to see how abstracting arguments from their contexts can lead to an ideological interpretation of the actual practice of philosophy as an exercise in pure thought. The decision between these two notional stances cannot be made in terms of either stance itself, and it is this situation which needs to be confronted when pondering the relation between philosophy and its histories. As Adorno sometimes argues (particularly in his lectures), it is sometimes best to regard a philosophical contradiction as an expression of a historical tension that cannot be resolved within philosophy. The danger here, which Adorno does not always avoid, lies in laying claim to a metaphilosophical position which would explain the contradiction in its terms. It is precisely because the terms of a philosophical debate always have more implications than we can become aware of that we need to build in the tension outlined here into the practice of philosophy.

103

References

Habermas, Jürgen (1999) *Wahrheit und Rechtfertigung*, (Frankfurt: Suhrkamp)

Pinkard, Terry (1996) *Hegel's Phenomenology. The Sociality of Reason*, (Cambridge: Cambridge University Press)

Pippin, Robert (1999) *Modernism as a Philosophical Problem*, (Oxford: Blackwell)

Putnam, Hilary (1983), *Realism and Reason. Philosophical Papers Vol. 3.* Cambridge: Cambridge University Press

Rorty, Richard (1989) *Contingency, Irony, and Solidarity*, (Cambridge: Cambridge University Press)

Rorty, Richard ed., (1992) *The Linguistic Turn*, (Chicago: University of Chicago Press)

Rorty, Richard (1998) *Truth and Progress*, (Cambridge: Cambridge University Press)

Rorty, Richard (1999) *Philosophy and Social Hope*, (Harmondsworth: Penguin)

Schlegel, Friedrich (1988) *Kritische Schriften und Fragmente 1–6*, (Paderborn: Schöningh)

THE IRRELEVANCE OF 'CONTINENTAL PHILOSOPHY'

With a few honorable exceptions, like the early Romantics, Nietzsche, and Derrida, it is all too rare for modern philosophers to remember that if philosophy is a practice, success in that practice may come about in more indirect ways than by making claims to be assessed by one's peers. Sometimes it is better to say things which aim at eliciting a reaction, rather than being taken at face value. The following piece provoked some scandalised reactions from people who are otherwise very keen on the idea of the literary status of philosophy and on philosophical 'play'. To this extent, the paper succeeded in doing what I wanted it to. I got a similar reaction when I once gave a paper on Nietzsche to a group of Nietzsche fans which was as rude about him as he is about other philosophers. The only names mentioned in what I have to say will be so canonical that if their bearers are still alive they ought not to be offended. If you think you are being talked about, that will therefore be your judgement, not mine. It may be that I am really talking about myself.

There probably was a time when doing 'Continental Philosophy' was something of a novel and heroic enterprise,[9] both in this country and America. Given present-day employment prospects, a certain degree of heroism is undoubtedly still required for those just beginning, but the heroism of intellectual novelty is a thing of the past, and we are now seeing distinct signs of stagnation. What we all used to hate (and in many ways still do) about much of the analytical tradition was its concern with problems whose solution would not make a blind bit of difference to anybody but the person whose article proposed the next move in the futile

---

[9] I use the term 'Continental Philosophy' here, not because I generally approve of it – I prefer 'European' – but because that is the term usually employed in relation to the style of philosophising I am concerned about.

game, and to those who were upset at having to give up some cherished views when their moves were superseded. 'Do numbers really exist?', and such questions, evidently still do concern far too many people who need to get a life. However, these questions have now been joined by a whole series of equally pointless reflections on minute intertextual moves in which the same cast of Hegel, Nietzsche, Heidegger, Adorno, Bataille, Lyotard, Derrida, et al. are shuffled in relation to each other in order to articulate just what it is that Continental philosophy uniquely has to say about our situation that nothing else can. Now I think there was a time when hybridising ('reading x with y') two or more of these figures was probably quite a fun thing to do, but these days it is getting very tedious, and less and less people are listening. The fact is that much that is argued in this connection relies on a series of 'Continental' shibboleths which now need serious scrutiny.

One obvious example here is the arrogance of using the more than debatable views of Heidegger on the Gestell, or Horkheimer and Adorno's Dialectic of Enlightenment, to diagnose a crisis which in Heidegger's case only post-philosophical 'thinking' is able even to begin to reveal. Now either the story about Western metaphysics as the domination of being by the subject is correct, in which case all aspects of human life in modernity have to be read in terms of it, or it needs to be argued about with people from every conceivable other discipline, from physics, to history, to sociology as just one other approach to the issue of modernity. Does anyone, though, actually set about doing this? If one accepts the extreme version of Heidegger's story one presumably feels as though one has joined an exclusive élite who are in on something nobody else can understand, so that one is able to talk about 'the history of the West' or the 'universal context of delusion' from a position which, while supposedly deconstructing a dominant totality, seems to be able to stand outside what it is deconstructing. Now I'm not saying that either Heidegger or Adorno was unaware of the difficulties this gave rise to, but merely adopting their assumptions as a way of understanding our world is simply a mark of intellectual cravenness. On what basis does one adopt such a view in the first place? It is no good pointing to Auschwitz, Hiroshima, and all the other standard examples of the horrors created by technological civilisation, because there are plenty of other approaches to understanding the unimaginable horrors in modernity which do not rely on a projection of a bit of the history of philosophy onto history as a whole. The further danger of this story is that it turns contingency into fate, because it offers no practical suggestions as to what would make such events impossible in the future. You can learn more about that from watching Shoah than doing philosophy.

Another favourite way of being a Continental philosopher, which derives from much the same source, results from 'subverting the subject' so enthusiastically that the subject is regarded as only 'spoken' by its language, or 'constituted' by, or 'inserted into' its discourse, or whatever. Now does anyone proposing such a view have any difficulty with the fact that they are putting it forward via a piece of communicative action which presumably subverts their reasons for proposing it? Why is it that the most grandiose egotists in Continental philosophy are usually those most concerned to render 'the subject' the effect of something else? This is not to say that the subject's relation to language is one of transparent control, but it is to question why ideas about the subject's almost total power-lessness are so popular these days. I have no doubt that one of the tasks of a critical philosophy is to propose different ways of talking about things which will make our relation to them and to each other less coercive, but without some conception of agency which reveals the admittedly limited possibilities of refusing to talk in the dominant manner, we once again join the élite who know so much better.

Let's take another area of still too often unquestioned consensus. Not many Continental philosophers in this country would admit to being a causal realist who thinks that scientific theories are, if not yet actually representations of how the world is as seen from nowhere, at least on the way to being this, and that language is not a central issue in the sciences.

As you probably know, Chris Norris has broken ranks, and many others are moving into the Critical Realist camp, and one can see why they might: what solves problems more obviously than anything else are the methods of modern science. Yes, they also create possibly terminal problems as well, but I have yet to see a theory which suggests a serious positive alternative to the scientific methods we already have, which in one sense already make the realists' case for them. I say this as one who does not consider himself a realist (or an anti-realist) and who, somewhat like Rorty, thinks the realism/anti-realism debate is probably pointless, on the assumption that it is usually merely silly to question, as Rorty puts it – thereby attempting to circumvent the issue of realism – that predictions turn out more reliably if we talk about x in the following scientifically established manner. The really important point here is that if there is one area in which Continental philosophy might have a serious social role to play, it is as a potential resource for questioning the scientism which has now become the dominant norm in the media, and which affects government priorities in education, the health service, and most other areas of contemporary life. Is this the dominant focus of work in recent Continental philosophy in this country? Do we see Continental philosophers lining up to show Richard Dawkins what a rubbish metaphysician he is? I don't think so. Furthermore, even if it were the dominant focus, it would probably have no effect, because the audience it needs to reach would wonder what on earth these people were talking about.

Now I think it is regrettable that the ideas of Adorno, Foucault et al are only common currency in a few institutions of higher education, but the important issue is why, given that they have now been around for long enough, they continue to be largely ignored or rubbished by those who might be persuaded that they offer a dimension of reflection which has been otherwise lacking in the public debate. One simple reason is the damaging assumption that to do Continental philosophy properly one has to write as though one were really writing an English version of a French text which is itself based on dubious translations of Heidegger. If it is the case that these ideas cannot survive without the obscure vocabulary and syntax, then the ideas are doomed to remain socially ineffective, and I think that would be a shame.

Another issue here also relates to the dubious relationship to the natural sciences of too many Continental philosophers. Why do so many people in Continental philosophy take psychoanalysis so seriously, when it is becoming obvious that it is, as a therapeutic practice, often (but not always – I have no doubt that there are good psychoanalytical therapists, though whether the theory is the basis of their success is another matter) the doctrine of medically untrained charlatans, based on a largely discredited philosophy of mind? – The notion of the unconscious as used by some Freudians makes no sense, for example, given that some level of consciousness must always be involved for the questionable idea of 'repression' even to become an issue. – There are insights into questions about the subject in psychoanalysis which can be argued about in relation to the questions of self-consciousness which began with Augustine, were developed to a great degree of sophistication by the German Romantics, and which now concern the analytical philosophy of mind. However, as a therapeutic practice, psychoanalysis congenitally resists validation and is often largely redundant, if not in some cases, damaging, assuming it is even clear just what that practice now is. In last week's Observer a psychoanalyst tried to suggest that other therapeutic techniques (many of which have been shown to work) did not get people to look at the really deep and difficult issues, as though most people were not aware of such issues and needed an analyst to tell them about them. This can be the case, but the claim to have privileged access to such issues is fraught with dangers. Within any academic subject there is a tendency for the dominant perspective to lead those in the subject to seek confirmation only from within, on the basis that those outside don't understand, because they haven't seen the light, or done the training. When a subject is as institutionally weak as European philosophy in this country, this is a disastrous assumption, and hitching one's wagon uncritically to psychoanalysis can only speed the decline which already threatens to overtake all aspects of Continental philosophy.

One final example: we need to come to terms with the 'feudal Germany' /'Vienna Congress' aspect of Continental philosophy. As was the case during the Revolutionary period in Germany, and after the Napoleonic era all over Europe, the degree to which thought was politically ineffective relates directly to the degree of speculative fantasy and to the over-production of theory. It may be that this also led to the greatest music of all time, and this is not to be taken lightly, but this was also a result of so many other factors that it is a dubious model for the present. As Rorty shows in his recent book on America, the concerns of the theoretical Left have led, at a time of the ascendancy of the Right, to a completely diminished input into the mainstream of politics, and the same is true of much of the post-1968 theorising that bears the name Continental Philosophy in this country. While, as Rorty suggests, the degree of sadism against the other has diminished in certain areas of American and British society via the concern with integrity of 'the other' and with identity politics, inequalities have massively increased, because the Left took its eye off the politico-economic ball. The very idea of talking about the 'possibility of politics' suggests the absurdity here: the people in power don't have this sort of discussion. Furthermore, all the talk in the world about the ethics of alterity cannot conceal the fact that in our actual negotiations with others there is a necessary degree of aggression and symbolic 'violence' which nothing is going finally to abolish. (Psychoanalysis seems to have this much right, at least.) Indeed, too much Continental philosophy assumes that argument is itself violent and therefore to be avoided. The obsession with the futile attempt to obviate symbolically mediated 'violence' has arguably played at least some role in an increase in the sources of real physical violence based on poverty, exclusion etc. I am not saying the symbolic dimension is not vital – in one sense it is, of course, all we have got in politics – but I am saying that we need to reflect in new ways upon the relationship between

the symbolic and the economic spheres, without diminishing the role of
the latter as part of what determines which ideas get adopted. Marx, as
more and more people are beginning to realise, is not dead. (Over ten
years on from the writing of this paper, the need to develop what is still
alive in Marx is ever more pressing.)

In a rant like this, it is easy to mix lots of different issues together, and I
think this is sometimes a good idea. However, I'll now try to clarify a few
of the options that I think ensue from what I have said. Philosophy is, like
it or not, an academic subject, and it is doomed to irrelevance if it does not
take this into account. As someone once actually said to me, referring to his
own institution, the 'hegemonic discourse here is analytical philosophy'.
How does one change a hegemony? Well, it becomes rather easier when
the dominant discourse is actually leaving the door open, as the growing
interest in the history of subject among analytical philosophers shows.
At the same time, the door often rapidly closes again, because styles of
philosophy differ so greatly that much of the analytical camp cannot see
beyond its own ways of arguing. We need therefore to establish much
more effectively on which terrain the battles should be fought. It is no
good, for example, competing at the level of the most technical questions,
as many German philosophers who are now trying to turn themselves
into rigorous analytical philosophers regularly find out by being ignored
in America. We can only really cooperatively compete at the level of re-
contextualisation, thus of the historicisation which is now becoming part
of the most significant analytical philosophers' reflections. This involves,
for example, telling a lot of new stories about the history of philosophy
and about the exclusions occasioned by the ignorance of those stories in
the analytical canon. The fact is that the number of unread major thinkers
remains far too great. If we wish to contest the validity of the very terrain
itself, then we must carry out cogent critiques of what the dominant
style of philosophy has actually done to the subject by removing so many
important philosophical questions from the agenda. This also becomes
a very practical issue about how subject divisions are located in the

humanities, in that, while philosophy departments have been severely reduced in number, what belongs within philosophy is done, often badly, in literature and other departments.[10] We need strategies for deciding how these divisions can be practically contested, given the resistance within subjects to incursions from outside.

The need to generate new stories is also urgent because the Continental canon in this country is much too limited. The main reason for this is linguistic: too many texts have not been translated, and many have been translated that we could happily have done without. Initiatives in this area are sorely needed, and we cannot expect help from publishers, unless extra finance is supplied from elsewhere. The other reason is ideological: many of the best philosophers are often dismissed on the sort of grounds cited above, as though we had already dealt with all that. A philosopher as important as Karl-Otto Apel, for example, gets translated, if at all, in obscure presses that go out of business, when the latest self-indulgent irrelevance by other philosophers is immediately translated. The market is doing significant damage here, and the way the subject is at present conspires with this. We therefore need a translation network which can get subsidies: this cannot be carried by one institution. The limitation of the canon goes along with the fear of the analytical Other that defines 'world philosophy' at present. As long as we see ourselves as separate from the mainstream of what goes on in philosophy people are still going to be encouraged, for example, to indulge in the sort of Heideggerese that is so popular in universities in the Deep South of America, where the fact that Ernst Tugendhat has arguably shown that there is no unified question of being is about as likely to affect the way Heidegger is written about as the Klu Klux Klan is to let African Americans join the club. (One should add, as Albrecht Wellmer has suggested, that the lack of a unified meaning of being may in fact be the crucial point in Heidegger's explorations.)

---

[10] Things have improved in the last ten years with regard to numbers in philosophy departments, though the analytical dominance continues.

Language need not always be argumentative or strategic, it can indeed be world-disclosive, and that can entail great difficulties of comprehension, but is everybody supposed to be the late Hölderlin when they write, or might the awfulness of their style not just be a result of their being beguiled by a somewhat bizarre, and very local short-lived tradition? A very simple initial suggestion that might help here is just to establish a list of words that are proscribed in certain contexts. On my list (taken from a Continental philosophy book I picked at random) would be 'site', 'excess', substantifications like 'the unique', 'the undecidable', 'originary', 'originary violence', 'violence' for acts of rudeness rather than physical acts, hyphenated items, 'circuit', 'rupture' (out of respect for the old), 'suture' (for similar reasons), 'zone', 'discourse' when one has not troubled to ponder whether one could actually give a description of the boundaries of what you are talking about, 'the language of metaphysics', because it is a silly idea, 'passage', because it is potentially rude, and so on. What these words now mean is 'I am doing Continental philosophy and have given up even thinking both about whether these words really do any work and about whether they might not lose me quite a large part of my audience'.

To conclude: I don't think there is now any deeper sense in using the term Continental philosophy, and using it as a label gives many people an excuse to ignore it. What we need to examine is which forms of philosophy address and potentially offer answers or new approaches to real questions which are not adequately covered in other disciplines, whether these are questions to do, for example, with aspects of self-consciousness not explained by cognitive science, aesthetic questions that undermine reductionist accounts of the real, or questions which show the need for a historical dimension which makes us ask why we think x is an interesting philosophical problem. At the moment one will get more in this respect from reading Thomas Nagel (whose latest book I loathe, but which at least forces one to respond), or Richard Rorty, than from most of the work in Continental philosophy produced in this country (and most of what was produced in America) in recent years.

Although Continental philosophy has done important work in revealing the vital hermeneutic dimension to dealing with all philosophical texts, it has also tended to introduce 'special text' status for its own canon, to the point where asking about the truth of the special text or its place in contemporary debates beyond philosophy nearly always gets forgotten in the name of establishing its relations to the other canonical texts or in working out yet another way in which we can try to make sense of a particularly obscure but exciting passage. We must, simply, be more concerned with the argumentative dimension of our understanding of texts than has tended to be the case, while at the same time guarding against the analytical failure to realise that arguments are always in some ways context-dependent for their significance. We must also be much more clearly and overtly aggressive in relation to deep failings in the analytical tradition to which there are important answers in the Continental tradition. Given the growing disintegration of the project of a theory of meaning, for example, the reminder that the reasons for that failure were already clearly stated in the first half of the 19th century by the German Romantics might help force the opening of horizons between the traditions which seems to me the only way forward if both sides of philosophy as it is done at present are to find the new approaches that will sustain the subject in the future. Finally, the idea of 'European philosophy', independent of analytical, hermeneutic, phenomenological orientation will be a vital political issue in the coming years, and we need to do something about it.